Down
to
the
Top

To my wife V, the angel at my side...

And Sonny, my brother, who walked with me through the valley of
the shadow of death...

Contents

1. The story of David
2. Let's back up
3. What happened when I got home
4. Last year of junior school
5. High school
6. I should have died
7. Solutions
8. Moving on
9. Deeper
10. Snowballs
11. Charles
12. Problems
13. Gone
14. Ecstacy
15. The other side
16. Random memories
17. Good times
18. The end of that
19. Busted
20. Even deeper
21. Ready to leave
22. Jerusalem
23. Tel Aviv
24. Cleaning up

25. House party

26. The hustler

27. Sonny

28. David and Sonny

29. Checking out

30. Back

31. A second job

32. Brief South African visit

33. Sonny's story

34. Grace

35. Mozambique

36. My life is in your hands

37. Living

38. Leaving again

39. Land of the free

40. The thief

41. The serpent

42. More balls

43. Biological mother

44. Wasting away

45. The helicopter

46. Freedom

Author's note

The clouds

How to fill the house

Distant deity

Some words from David

Proverbs 23

You shall strike him with the rod

and rescue his soul from Sheol...

1:
The Story of David

Hi, I'm David. I'm 12 years old and I'm sitting in a jail cell. I'm so scared I can taste it. Like some kind of gas or vapour at the back of my mouth. And that, I'm-about-to-bite-a-lemon feeling in my jaw. The cell feels damp. Damp and dark. It smells of other people's body excretions. Piss and sh*t and vomit. Probably a lot of sweat. Fear sweat.

The police have just taken my friend to the next room. It was quiet for a moment. Then I heard a crack, followed by an excruciating scream. More cracks and the scream turned to broken sobs. As if his mind could not make the connection between the pain and the expression of it.

I knew that I was next. My friend was 16. I was only 12. The taste of fear increased. Incredibly enough, along with that fear come a different feeling. Something new. I didn't know what it was exactly. Now I know it was pride and determination.

A really big policeman came into my cell. He had red hair. He was a giant. He was an angel of doom. He was here to introduce me to his wrath. Somehow I managed to walk without my knees giving way.

He told me to take my pants down. I felt so vulnerable. The taste of fear was so much I felt as if I could vomit it out. I braced myself. I knew it was going to be bad. The first crack of that cane sent excruciating pain throughout my entire body. You'd think it would only hurt where it landed. But that is not how it is. Literally, every nerve in my body felt that crack. I wanted to scream. 'One is enough. I have learned my lesson! One is enough!'

But I was getting 4! There was no way I was going to scream or cry in front of this man! I could tell he was surprised at my silence. He muttered under his breath, 'So you are a tough one are you?'

The second crack I felt my skin split open. It was so bad. I had to bite into my lip so I wouldn't scream out loud. The angel of doom was even more surprised at the silence that remained in the room.

I could hear his breathing. He seemed to be just as determined to make me scream as I was to remain quiet. The third crack. I could feel the blood running down my legs. I bit so hard on my lip. I could taste the blood in my mouth now too. In my mind, I called him every filthy name under the sun. I used my anger to sustain my determination.

My pain sensors were unable to acknowledge the fourth crack. My adrenaline was in overdrive.

When it was over the angel of doom spoke, "You are going to be a troublemaker. I can tell. Good luck to you kid. You are tough as nails."

Two things happened at that moment. He prophesied over my future and I had gained his respect.

I didn't want or need either!

Exodus 20

Thou shalt not steal...

2:
Let's Back Up

So how did I end up in that terrible predicament? Well, it was easier than you think. I lived in a small town in South Africa. My family didn't have a lot of money but we got by.

My best friend Deon was 16. Unlikely I know. But it happened. After school on Fridays, we would go to the local supermarket and shoplift. It was great fun. I was quite good at it. It was also cool just to have stuff. Stuff we never would have had because we couldn't afford it. We would challenge each other. Our tokens of rebellion grew in size. We thought that we were invincible. Until one day we weren't.

I strolled out of that store without a care in the world. And then my life changed for good. From '...get those kids...' to the police station... to fingerprinting... to getting a court date set. Waiting the entire holiday for sentencing. Like that wasn't bad enough, but there was something more in store. And I was going to find that out when I got home.

There was no summer holiday, carefree break. My world crashed down. Everything I ever knew to be the truth changed. You'd think that being caught stealing would wake me up. Make me scared enough to want to be good. Scared enough to stop breaking the law.

Enough for this young man to say 'Okay, lesson learned. No more shoplifting' But what happened when I got home turned it all around. My rebellious nature was watered to the brim. Fuel was added to that fire and it blazed something awful.

Psalm 27

For my father and my mother have forsaken me,

but the Lord will take me in

3: What Happened When I Got Home

"You are not my son….that is why you behave this way!"

What? What? My mother. My own flesh and blood. My mommy is not my mother?

It's a crazy thing to hear 12 years after the fact. Maybe it wasn't 12 years. Maybe I was 1 or 2 when she adopted me. I tried to question her but she blew it off. Trying to pretend she had only said it in anger. But I knew deep inside myself that it was the truth.

Along with that truth comes so much burden. And so many questions. And there is nothing worse than questions with no answers when it comes to your very own existence.

I hated everyone and everything. How could punishment for shoplifting be brutal violence? Literally getting the skin flayed off your body! I needed to come home to some kind of love after getting beaten like that. I needed a mother's, unconditional love. I needed someone to tell me it was going to be okay. They would be with me every step of the way. But the opposite happened.

And now I am disowned! I don't actually belong here. The only reason I am here is that these people felt sorry for me. I am a pity child.

I knew deep down that this was not the whole truth but it was the only part of the truth I could see at the time. The biggest impact of that news was that I felt alone. I was 12 years old and I stood alone.

Going back to school was interesting. I could not sit. I literally could not sit. The benches were so hard and my rear end needed more time to heal. I'd try and sit to the side, but both sides were flayed.

My shorts stuck to my skin. If I sat too long they would somehow grow together. Then later I would have to peel them apart. I even try to pretend to be sitting and keep my body weight on my legs. But that was such hard work. Too hard, my legs were not strong enough. Everything was a challenge. Every day was a challenge!

Deon and I never breathed a word of it to anyone. We didn't discuss it with each other either. I wondered if his ass was also sticking to his shorts. Maybe they weren't. He did scream. Maybe they didn't hit him as hard. Maybe I should have screamed.

We suffered in silence. This cemented our bond. He took me into his circle of friends. They were all so much older than me. I have two vivid memories of first times.

"Hey, kid" that was one of Deon's friends "do you smoke?"

Me, "Sure I do." I had never smoked in my life.

He handed me the cigarette and I became a smoker.

"Hey kid" another of Deon's friends "do you drink?"

Me, "Sure I do."

A whole lot of Old Brown Sherry later I was lying face down in a vomit-filled flower bed.

This was the introduction to my life of substance abuse. It was the introduction to the man I would one day become.

2 Corinthians

We have renounced the things hidden because of shame

4:
Last Year of Junior High School

After the summer break, I started my last year of junior school. Summer had been hard. The subject of adoption was taboo. And my mind continually returned to the same questions.

Who was my real mother?

What did she look like?

Did I look like her?

Did I have siblings?

Did I belong to anyone?

Did anyone love me unconditionally?

Would I always have to feel rejected?

I couldn't help it. I felt like I didn't belong in my own life and I wanted to have a life where I did belong. I couldn't find a shape to close the empty hole inside of me. So I just had to live with it.

During the week I would just get on with it. I went to school. I played rugby and cricket after school. And I was good at it. Played first team. But it really was just getting on with it. My life was all about the weekends.

Weekends meant getting away from my life. Getting away from my mind. Getting away from my gaping hole. A bottle of Gin will do that you know. Unfortunately, it only works for a little while. It's not magic. It wears off. But of course, I would just go back and get more.

In a way, it was quite surreal. Being at school with all these 'normal' 12-year-olds. When I look back at it now, I cannot believe that I was only 12. Twelve is just a kid. The other kids were just kids.

And there I was, trying to get on with it. In my upside down, back to front, mess of a life.

On the upside. I was very popular with the girls. I guess it's true what they say. The ladies really do like the bad boys.

The problem is that I was too young for all of it. Back then I thought I was cool. I thought I was tough. I thought I was doing a pretty good job of it. Considering my circumstances. Now, of course, I know that I was unable to process anything.

Everything was going in and nothing was being processed. The hill was turning into a mountain!

Proverbs 29

...a child left to himself brings shame to his mother....

5:
High School

"Hey, you!" Assembly had just finished. "You with the hair!" The voice was loud and clear. Of course, I know he was speaking to me. I had been expecting it.

"You with the weird haircut, get to my office right now!"

Yup! I was the one with the weird haircut. I had grown it all summer only to shave it into a mohawk the day before high school started. I wanted to stand out. I wanted everyone to know there was no messing with me.

"You apologise for the disrespect and sort that hair out after school today!" He was really angry. I just stood and looked at him.

"Did you not hear me, young man. I said apologise!" His face was getting rather red.

I remained quiet. I would never say sorry. I was my hair. I could do what I wanted with it.

He proceeded to rant and rave and fill the room with threats. Still, I remained quiet.

3 Lashes later I was allowed to leave.

The physical pain was nothing compared to the respect I had gained with my peers. They were pussy lashes anyway. Nothing like that prick policeman.

There would be no initiation for me. No one would bully me. The friends I made were all years ahead of me. I was way ahead of the game. That older crowd turned out to be the beginning of my downward spiral into the life of addiction.

When I was 15 I got a motorbike. Legally I was required to be 16. But it was close enough. I wasn't one to nit-pick about these little details. The bike changed my life. It represented freedom. I came and went as I pleased. It was awesome. I liked to take my helmet off so I could feel the wind, feel the freedom.

I clearly remember visiting a friend one Saturday afternoon.

In South Africa, marijuana is called dagga and a pipe usually refers to a broken off bottleneck. It's what we smoked our dagga from.

My friend's brother was in the little shack in the garden. He called me.

"Hey, Dave, come and give me a light man."

I'd done this many times before. I light 2 matches while he sucks on the bottleneck. I never really felt the effects of dagga. I didn't get the chance to smoke it that often.

But this time things didn't go as I expected. He sucked on the pipe. Then he killed the glowing burn with the back of a matchstick. After that, he pulled a piece of paper out of his pocket. The paper contained some white powder. He poured half this powder on to the surface of the pipe.

I gave him another light. A sweet stinky smell filled the room. Little did I know that smell would become my true romance. My love-hate relationship for years and years to come. He took a hit and then passed it to me.

"Have a hit man." It sounded more like one word than a sentence. He was slurring and drooling a bit.

I took the pipe and sucked that white smoke deep into my lungs.

I left the room in a rush. I went into the clouds. Heavy black thunderclouds. Inviting me in. I drifted into nowhere land. In nowhere land nothing is constant and nothing is real. Well, except for the reality of nowhere. In nowhere land, everything happened in slow motion. I was sitting in the school ground talking to Deon. Then I wasn't. I was working on my bike with my dad. Then I wasn't. I focused a bit. My nowhere land friend was sitting next to me.

"Hey man." I smiled at him.

"Hey." He slurred.

We were in the same place but we didn't meet. We were together but we were drifting on different planes, different clouds. For the next hour, we came and went. Visiting places inside our heads only we knew about.

I fell in love for the first time that day. I fell in love with the sweet stench of oblivion.

Psalm 10

But you have seen, for you observe trouble and grief,

to repay it by your hand.

The helpless commits himself to you.

You are the helper of the fatherless.

6:
I Should Have Died

I made more nowhere land friends. This was my crowd. We wanted the same things. It made sense. One weekend we decided to go to a club just outside of town. They required no I.D. and you could bring your own booze.

We didn't have booze, so we stole it from our father's cabinets. We didn't have a car so we 'borrowed' one from a parent. I remember getting to the club and thinking 'okay just act like you have been coming here all your life.'

We were all having a good time getting pretty drunk. I guess I wasn't getting pretty drunk. I was completely hammered. Hammered beyond the ability to retain memories.

I went to the toilet... And then I was sitting with my friends at the table. I looked down and I could see a lot of blood.

"David, are you okay?" One of my drunk friends.

"Yeah man, I'm good," I answered.

But I wasn't good. That was a sh*t load of blood. I needed some fresh air. I could not really tell if I was okay or not. My head was spinning from the booze.

When I got outside I lay down. I don't know how long I had been lying there.

"We have to help him," a woman's voice.

"I don't want to get involved, let's just leave him. Someone else will help." A man's voice.

"What if he dies before someone else notices him? We have to do something!" The same woman.

They dragged me into their car. It was a long ride. I was bleeding all over the car. When we got to the hospital the man told me to get out. I did the best I could. The car sped off.

He was obviously serious about not wanting to get involved. But at least I was at a hospital. I still didn't know what was going on. All I knew is that I was bleeding from somewhere.

"Get him on the stretcher. He has lost a lot of blood, we need to move!" A male voice.

Then a doctors voice "Stitch him up, and don't worry about making it pretty. This guy is not going to make it."

They hooked up a bag of blood and left me.

When they asked for my name I said John Ashton. But my friends had been looking for me and finally found me. Apparently, I had got into a fight with too many guys in that bathroom. They beat me into the urinal which broke and stabbed me in the kidney area. Crazy! I had no recollection of this.

Quite a large part of that urinal must have pierced my body because I was told you could fit a hand into the wound.

Well, my friends gave my real name and eventually, my father came to fetch me. He didn't say a word but his eyes told me everything. This adopted boy was a huge disappointment to him.

1 Corinthians 15

...Bad company corrupts good character...

7: Solutions

I was given two weeks worth of pain medication. I doubled the dose and swallowed them down with brandy. This eased the physical pain as well as the screaming silence that had filled our home.

Needless to say, the meds didn't last long. I needed my sweet white pipe. My friends were happy to hook me up after the ordeal I had been through. But of course, this could not go on forever. I needed a way to fund my first love.

That sweet white pipe is Mandrax. It was initially brought on to the market by a French pharmaceutical company called Rousselle Laboratories. After they realised how highly addictive the substance was, it was banned from the market in 1977. To this day it remains one of the most widely used drugs in South Africa.

Mandrax can be injected, swallowed or snorted. But the most common way it is used is to crush it up and smoke it with dagga.

In the time of my youth, South Africa was still an apartheid country. White people and black people were segregated. We lived separately. I remember all the 'whites only' signs. On toilet doors, on park benches.

Black people lived in tin shack communities outside of town. They were called locations. It was in these locations that I found my source of income. They sold me dagga for a good price. I then sold it for a better price.

White people did not go into the locations. White people got killed in the locations. Initially, they tolerated me. Eventually, I had friends there. I guess they thought I was crazy. I'd bend the number plate on my bike so the cops would not be able to read it if they spotted me. I'd ride through the locations shirtless and high as a kite. I was absolutely fearless. I thought that the two knives I carried would save my life if it came down to it. Fortunately, it never came down to it.

Mind you, I had my fair share of fights. Just nothing life-threatening. The place was filled with prostitutes of every shape size and colour. I remember once a guy was giving the ladies a hard time. I broke a beer bottle over his head. I didn't think about it, I was high anyway. I just picked the bottle up and smashed it into his head. The ladies were so grateful I ended up doing a double with them.

Your mind went straight into the gutter there didn't it? A double is not sexual. A double is smoking two pills at once. A double sends you to Mars. To the twilight zone. And it keeps you there for hours.

1 Peter 5

Be sober-minded, be watchful.

8:
Moving On

I have heard that dagga is supposed to be the gateway drug. The so-called experts say that if you smoke weed you will be more inclined to do other drugs. I am here to tell you that right there is some B.S.

The truth is, you are either the kind of person who likes drugs or not. I know tons of people who tried it all and never liked it. But I am not one of them.

And I don't just like it, I love it. I love the altered state of mind. I love the oblivion. I was only just getting started. I was about to try something that would seriously f**K my mind up.

I was out with a few friends and current girlfriend. It was a seriously seedy joint. Very specific crowd. Bikers and users. My girlfriend was speaking to a couple of guys. They were from Johannesburg, Hillbrow. The hardcore of hardcores. She comes back over to me.

"Babe, they got acid. Want to try some?"

So I'm talking to them.

"What you got man?"

Hardcore says "they are double-dipped, take it easy, maybe a quarter."

I took the little square piece of paper from him "Do I look like a f***kin pussy?" Swallowed the entire thing.

I carried on playing pool and nothing happened. Double-dipped my ass. I even went back to the guys and told them they sold me a dud.

He smiled and said, "give it time man."

I took my lady friend home and then headed home myself. It was a warm evening and I was just cruising on my bike.

F**k the street lights looked pretty funky. Red light. Orange light. White light. Red. Orange. White. Long red. Long red. All the lights together. Christmas trees. Kaleidoscopes.

Wait, what am I doing? I need to focus. I'm on the road. There is other traffic. Concentrate. Concentrate.

Wait, what am I concentrating on?

I'm losing my sentences.

Mother F****ker, those lights are funky.

The road…..look…….road.

To this day I don't know how long it took me to get home that night. I could have been riding at snail's pace… or not.

Back home, in my room.

My room was dark. I had black curtains. Black candles. Posters of Goth bands. Evil sinister posters. I had drawn pentagrams all over the walls.

The darkness sucked me in. Evil engulfed me. The posters seemed alive. Images moving then keeping still. Trying to confuse me, haunt me….

Orange juice....orange juice......hold on to that thought! Orange juice. I drank a few glasses. Once somewhere I heard that orange juice kills trips.

Ok...sleep. Just sleep.

Get off me! Get off! What the f**k! I can't breathe. Stop choking me. I can't move. I'm paralyzed and I'm dying. Something is killing me.

Get the f**k off! I couldn't move. I couldn't fight it. What was it? Darkness...shadows...evil...demons.

The pressure around my neck was intense. I couldn't catch a breath, I could feel my eyes bulging...ready to burst...the posters were taunting me...they were encouraging my dark assailant...this is how I was going to die...

Finally, at some point, it seemed to lose some power. I could move again. I ran out of the house. My body was soaking in sweat. My heart was pounding in my ears.

I fought this evil until the sun came up. There are no words to tell what I went through that night. It was dark and it was terrifying.

I took a pill out of my pocket, crushed it and loaded that pipe. Finally, the nightmare was over. Finally, oblivious dark clouds took over. I left this evil place and went there. The other place that is not in this world.

Acid is a crazy drug. It opens doors in the mind that, in my opinion, should not be opened. The intense part is that you can never really close those doors again. Even when you are not tripping.

At some point or other, frequent acid users will probably have a 'bad trip.'

Inanimate objects all become alive. This is quite entertaining. But on a bad trip, this insanity plays against you instead of with you. I once watched a girl laugh at wallpaper for hours. The wallpaper had horses on it. To her, the horses were alive. It entertained her. But when my posters became alive it was sinister and evil.

On a bad trip, your mind can't form sentences. It can't hold a thought for long enough. You know something is wrong. Deep inside, you think you have gone crazy and you are going to stay that way.

I have heard hundreds of stories of bad trips. One guy told me it was the first time he dropped acid. He was at a rave and became paranoid. He went to the bathroom to try and get his head straight. He opened the tap to splash water on his face and pure blood came out of the taps. Everyone he watched in the bathroom used the taps. They were all splashing and drinking blood.

A girl once told e that she had dropped acid often. But one day she was tripping in the forest. She was lying on the ground between the tall trees. She lifted her arms and legs and pretended she was hanging off the earth. As if the ground were the top and the sky was the bottom. When she finally decided to get up, the world remained upside down. For the duration of the trip, the world remained inverted.

It takes a certain kind of person, with a certain kind of determination, to take acid again after a bad trip. I was that kind of person.

I reckon if one could imagine what hell is like, that would be it. A permanent bad trip.

Proverbs 13

...a companion of fools suffers harm...

9: Deeper

Through all of this, I was still attending school. I never bothered much with studying. Somehow I always did well. In fact, I finished school with a B average and I never opened a book. Not that anything I learned was going to help me. That education was for nothing. My university was on the streets. That is where I learned to sharpen my skills for the promotion I was about to give myself.

After school I attended college. I only went to placate my parents. In reality, all I was doing was selling drugs to the rich bored kids. A rasta friend and I would drive into the locations on Friday evenings. We would buy 3 or 4 black bags full of weed to distribute during the week.

On the way back from scoring we would hit the pipe in the car, blowing the smoke out of the windows without a care in the world.

I was earning a good living selling weed and buttons (mandrax) I was selling at college and hitting the club scene in the evenings. Anyone who needed anything knew me. There were plenty of women too.

I had a short relationship with a lovely lady. She was a few years older than me. Long red hair and porcelain skin. She taught me a thing or two. One-night-stands were not the same as being in a relationship. Relationships came with the luxury of time. Time to explore one another. I really enjoyed that. But unfortunately, I got bored quickly. I was always moving on after a few months.

At this point in my life, I was only about a year out of high school. But I had spent so many of my school years at the location or hanging at dealers houses. I was respected and would even go so far as to say I was liked.

I knew that if it came down to it, almost all of those guys would have my back. Those guys being the biggest gangsters in Cape Town. And as it turned out, many times it did come down to it.

A new face appeared on the scene at one of the nightclubs. It was a face that interested me. I was pretty much as hardcore as it got. But this guy was a different kettle of fish altogether. For starters, he was from Johannesburg. That's kind of like comparing Sun City (a small casino in South Africa) to Las Vegas.

This new guy didn't look hardcore. In fact, he was quite a pretty boy with a well-to-do English name, like Charles. His father was a millionaire and he was up to everything in the book. He had a lot of heat on him so he came to Cape Town to cool off.

People said he was crazy. He didn't look crazy but I wanted to find out for myself. Fortunately, we had a mutual friend so I was able to set up a get-together.

I remember the first time I went to his house like it was yesterday. A few people were there. People who lived with him. His girlfriend and two other guys. We chilled and smoked a few buttons. Even then I could see this guy wasn't right in his head. Buttons chill you out. After the rush, you actually feel quite mellow. But not this guy. He was fueled by anger and hate. He really had a case of the crazies.

The trouble was I needed him. I was making good money and doing quite well, but with him, I could make even more. My own drug habit was getting very expensive, to say the least.

Charles and his partner were bringing LSD in from Europe, Amsterdam mostly. They planned to take over the entire Cape Town market.

He wanted to see if I could put money where my mouth is, so he gave me 100 caps of acid to sell. I was back the next day with the money for 100 caps of acid. Needless to say, he was impressed. I was in. If only I knew what I was getting in to.

I was to distribute acid, ecstasy, and cocaine. At the same time, I was still selling weed and buttons.

The trouble with this kind of thing is that it snowballs quickly. You blink twice and you no longer recognise the world around you.

Proverbs 16

Pride goes before destruction

And a haughty spirit before stumbling

10: Snowballs

"Look man, you know I don't like that in here."

That was the owner of the nightclub. He had the power to veto anyone in or out of the place. I was so arrogant I did not even answer him. I did look him in the eye though. Just to remind him.

He carried on speaking to someone else in the room.

"That stuff is disgusting and it stinks, he is going to bring the heat in here one day." He was referring to my white pipe.

"Not much you can do." Someone answered.

Damn straight there was not much he could do. Charles had him in his pocket and I was Charles's top dog.

At the beginning of the evening, a bunch of kids would come to see me and get their stash. They would then go off to the various nightclubs and distribute it. Some would pay up front, some took on consignment. I trusted them all. None of them had the balls to cross me. I always stayed at home base. This club was ours. It's like we owned it. We certainly owned the patrons and the women.

The thing is being a high roller is not without. Paranoia and stress are your constant companions. I got myself a bodyguard. Doesn't hurt to have eyes on the back of your head. You just never know.

What you have to understand is that at the beginning of an evening I would get in my car, drive to the nightclub. Walk from my car to the nightclub. During this simple process, I had 1000 caps of acid, 1000 E's and at least 100 grams of coke on me. It was like a game of walk the plank every single night. Heartbeat elevated. Fear pressing in. The enormous relief when entering the door of safety.

One more night that I didn't fall off the end and drown. Between the cops and anyone who might want to reap the financial benefits of that amount of gear, I was literally a walking target.

In order to combat all that stress and paranoia, I self-medicated. Buttons to chill out. Coke to motivate myself and alcohol to take the edge off. My day looked something like this.

Wake up. Two beers to take the edge off the night before. They were never enough so a couple of buttons. That always worked. Mess around the house for a bit. Drink another beer and have a shot of anything that was there. Eat some food. Realise that I have to go on a few missions. Collecting money or dropping stash. Do a few lines of coke to motivate myself for these missions.

Wherever the missions took me, I would inevitably end up sitting with someone topping up my state of mind. A few more buttons or some coke.

Head home. Sort out the stash for the night. Eat. Sleep for a few hours then head off to the club scene.

This was my life. Day in and day out.

This was my late teens and early 20's. Looking back now I can barely imagine it. But the body adapts. The truth is I would have fallen over without the stuff. I needed it physically. My body needed it to sustain any withdrawal symptoms.

John 10

The thief comes to steal and kill and destroy.

11: Charles

"Zippy is in jail bro" I was speaking to Charles. I lived with him now. Dropped out of college. Couldn't really see any point in it. And the bored white kids were small time. If they wanted anything, they knew where to find me.

"Which one is Zippy?" Charles asked after he snorted a massive line.

"The little crazy rasta," I answered "I knew it was a setup man. I told him. He said he knew the guy. Look where that got him."

Charles was pacing, he was wired. Seriously wired. "If I said it once I said it a thousand times. They all f***ing motherf***ers! Idiots! All of them! There is only one way to deal with them. F**k them up! Break bones! Beat them until all the stupid pieces fall out!"

He was getting wound up. Speaking too fast. Pacing. His 45 and 9mm were lying on the table in front of us as usual.

"And those dumb whores, don't even get me started on them!"

He sucked another huge line. Started agitatedly chopping a few more. Chop chop chop chop. Sniff sniff sniff sniff.

"Just like that stupid bi**ch upstairs! They all the same. Bunch of whores. She thinks she is something special." He was referring to his girlfriend upstairs.

He picked up his guns. I sat up. I had been chilling. Was in quite a haze myself. But whenever he started waving those guns around I woke up. Dragged myself out of my haze. Got on alert. The guy was wired and mad. I never really knew if he would pull that trigger.

When he got like this I would go through stages of survival in my mind. I looked at his face. He sure wasn't so pretty anymore.

I don't know if he was growing his hair and beard or if he just never bothered to shave anymore. Spit was flying out of his mouth while he ranted.

The next thing I knew the guy was on his way upstairs. Guns in hand.

Sh*t!

He started in on his girlfriend. Screaming and thuds followed. I knew he was hitting her. I could hear her crying for help. Man, this motherf***er sure knew how to kill a buzz.

I sat there for a while. F**k! He was Charles! What was I supposed to do now?

I took a bottle and went upstairs. I was hoping to reason with him. But needed a weapon just in case.

I knocked on the door a few times. They were so loud there was no way they could hear me. I opened the door. Her face was all blotchy and red. Her hair was a mess. Some of it was hanging a bit too long, I guess those bits were pulled out at the roots. She looked at me with desperation in her eyes. She actually looked a little funny, like someone had literally dragged her backwards through a bush.

Charles turned toward me and aimed. There was absolutely no hesitation in his eyes. My sphincter loosened then tightened. I closed the door again.

Sitting on the couch listening to the domestic violence. I slowly filled my pipe and crushed the white powder…….

………

That's better…..

Psalm 103

When the wind has passed, it is over and it is no more...

12: Problems

I thought my life was pretty good. I was earning up to two grand a day. I could afford my own habit and pretty much anything else I wanted. Even though the money went out just as quickly as it came in. There was always more where it came from. I had introduced Charles to all my gang connections. He was rather happy about that. It enabled him to get his coke locally and at wholesale prices.

We cut the coke so the customer only got 50% of the actual product, so mark up was decent. I did keep some of the good stuff for special customers and myself of course. Although I did coke and acid my main love was still Mandrax. She really was my one true romance. Even though I cheated on her all the time. Pretty much the same as the women in my life. I couldn't settle down.

They were interesting enough, to begin with, but inevitably I always got bored. Maybe it was because I was more off my face than I realized. I was separating sheets of acid on a daily basis. I never wore gloves. Who knows how much was going into my system? I definitely didn't live in the same world others did. Especially not in the same world as my lady friends. They came and went, some were very special. But even they could not keep my interest.

We got word that our club was going to close. This was not good news. We operated out entire business from there. It was ideal too. A big place, with a downstairs private area.

We would have to find another place to run our affairs. But this would cost money. Big money. Not to mention the loss we would make in the interim.

Although I have to say, what sticks in my mind from all of what was going on, was the closing down party. It lasted three days. Everyone knew the club was closing down. They were there to top up their stash for as long as it took. However long we needed to set up somewhere else. They were also there to say goodbye to their own private den of iniquity.

They all came here to escape. Some would escape to beautiful places. Others would end up in some kind of private hell. But no matter what...they always came back. And this was the last of it.

1 Corinthians 13

For now, we see only a reflection, as in a mirror

Then we shall see face to face

13:
Gone

I was about 48 hours in... no sleep...just more and more and more...

I didn't know if I was real or not. If I was awake or not. I lifted the pipe and took yet another hit.

Off I went...into the clouds...

I saw Tommy...hey Tommy...you're dead man...he looked good for dead...

Tommy used to hang out with a bunch of us. A friend of ours had a converted garage in the garden area. We called it the bunker. Tommy was one of us. Chilling, smoking, talking about everything and nothing. One day he stopped coming. But that was not all that unusual. People came and went in our world.

A few days later we found out why.

Tommy had gone to the location to score. Something bad went down. He was found with his tongue cut out and burned alive. That right there is hectic sh*t man. What a painful death that must have been. I try not to think about how much he must have screamed and begged for his life. And at what point he realized he was actually going to be burned alive. I don't even think being high would have helped.

I drifted back into the nightclub. Tried to take in my surroundings. Thought I saw Tommy. But it wasn't him. Some people actually still had the energy to move. These were the trippers and the coke-heads. Pupils so dilated their eyes were only black. The room was busy. Busy with people lying around or dancing around or floating around. I lifted my pipe again.

Into the clouds...I was having raunchy sex...someone's mother...her husband was watching...no...no...no...Tommy was watching...dead Tommy...

Came back for a bit. I felt like I needed to move. To see if I was alive. But I couldn't move. I did this to be lost. To hurt myself. To remind myself I can still feel. Now I didn't want to be lost. I wanted to come back. But I couldn't find myself.

Even in that state business was good. I made around 40 grand that weekend. Everyone stocking up. But that is not a lot of money when you are used to 2 grand a day coming in. I'd have to make it last until we sorted a new place.

1 Peter 4

The end of all things is near, therefore be of sound judgement...

14:
Ecstacy

The owner of our previous headquarters opened a new spot. The trouble is, it really was just a spot. Not a club. Just the kind of place people hang out. It was a much smaller place and there were just too many people, too many eyes. It didn't work for us. I was hustling on the street most of the time which was very dangerous. Between the cops and the competition, we needed a new place.

Things slowed down for a while. Which was cool except for the fact that my own habit was eating into my pocket. Eventually, we found a good spot which was much bigger and suited our purposes. Business was booming once again.

I remember one particular night. It was a slow night for a change. This chick starts in at me. 'Let do an E.'

Now I wasn't the kind of person to do pussy drugs like that. I always thought of them as soft. Anyway, the reason I do drugs at all is to shoot myself into oblivion. I never heard anyone say that E shot them into oblivion. It was all about feelings. Not my thing at all. Even I didn't know what I was feeling inside. I didn't need a drug to define that.

But this chick was persistent. So I relented.

I popped two. If you going to do it, do it right.

I was sitting at the bar counter waiting for my pills to kick in. The surface of the counter felt really smooth. I'd never noticed that before. I started rubbing my hand along the surface. It was so nice to touch, my hands just wanted more. Smooth, so smooth and cool. I looked around. The room was a warm haze of beautiful people. The candles are flickering warmth and light into the room.

The flames are leaping and dancing to the rhythmic music. Wax slowly creeps down the sides melting it back into itself. I'm enjoying the bar counter too much to move.

I watch my hands, they are melting too. They sink into the surface, the bar counter and I become one for a few moments. We provide the surface for the dancing candles spreading love.

A girl comes and leads me away from my counter, she leads me into a back room. She starts rubbing something minty all over my back. The touch of her hands feels like melting butter. Melting away my senses. The menthol smell opens my every receptor. I am one with the music, one with the crowd, one with myself. I'm cheating again. I think I'm in love with my new mistress.

Later I go back to my true romance, the combination of her and my mistress is incredible. Falling off the world in a dreamy haze. This combination was my new affair for quite some time.

Revelations 21

...he will wipe every tear from their eyes...

15:
The Other Side

I just want to take a short time out from my own story to tell about the other side of the coin.

My life was on the side of the gangs. I lived and hustled with them. It was extreme for me because I always had to think about my survival and safety. But the people, the innocent people suffered because of these gangs.

The Cape Flats is an area outside of Cape Town. It is a township that was created by the apartheid government in 1966. It was a cost-effective place for people of colour to live. These areas were most affected by gang violence.

Many gang members lived there, and they often lived on opposite sides of the same road. They would constantly shoot at each other. Regardless of who got in the way.

Mothers were terrified to send their children to school. Kids were terrified to walk to school. They would have to walk through gangs. Gangs that were shooting at each other. As a result, the children were running to school. They reported that they often did not know which way to run since the bullets were coming from every direction.

Every day normalities like going to school to the shops or just simply trying to get a haircut often ended with gunshot wounds or death.

No one did anything about it. The gangs were too powerful and everyone was too scared.

A 17-year-old girl was raped by two men. She decided to speak up. She decided that enough was enough. She wanted justice for what happened to her.

She identified the gang members who raped her. And she got her justice. They were imprisoned. It gave people hope for a while. For a moment it looked like just maybe a terrible crime would and could be punished.

This hope filled the newspapers and the television.

And then the girl was gunned down in public.

Hope died and crime prevailed.

It's horrific the way these innocent people were forced to live. The violence and death they dealt with every day. Because of gang politics and mentality that had nothing to do with them.

Proverbs 3

Do not envy a man of violence. And do not choose any of his ways.

16: Random Memories

The combination of buttons and E was always a tough comedown. It's like the E used up so much serotonin that your body needed tons of time to replace it. I was used to rough comedowns. But before it was just the physical push. Now it was physical and emotional. E always left me feeling like I was on a huge downer. Depressed almost.

I was lying on my bed in this state just thinking about my life. I had some booze and some weed to take the edge off. But that's all it did. Just the edge.

I never really bothered much with thoughts like 'what do I want from life.' Life was what it was. I hustled. That was my thing, my life. But the idea of a good woman appealed to me. I had my fair share of women, but mostly it always ended in so much drama it wasn't worth it.

Like this one chick, she was British. Not my usual type. But she was also adopted so we had that to bond us. Her parents gave her up because of drugs, so she hated drugs. But she did love drinking. It was good for a while but then she started coming down on me for my habit. One night we were on the way home from somewhere. I had no shirt or shoes. I was burning up from the pills and the buttons. She starts in at me. I'm wired enough from the drugs and she just kills my buzz. I end up chucking her out at home and speeding off. Only to total my car on the way to my spot. I hitch-hiked away from the wreck.

Another chick I had was a prostitute. She'd go to 'work' and then come back and we'd score whatever we wanted, get high and have sex ourselves. Was quite weird.

But she was really cool. She had her own story too, don't judge till you walked a mile. It worked out ok until her husband bust us. And I didn't even know she was married!

Then there was some messed up sh*t with a friends mother.

And of course, the model. Well, she was a model until she got messed up with buttons. She stopped modelling and started transporting for me. I remember one night the cops chased us. I chomped up the 6 pills I had one me. Ended up trying to fight them off, but the pills took over. Much later I woke up in the police station. They ended up letting me go.

The ex-model moved in with me. We were happy for a while. Man, don't get me wrong, that woman was greedy for her high. Cost me a small fortune. One time she had some sleazy friends visiting her, and after they left my stash was gone. Went straight to the guy's house and pistol-whipped him. Stash came safely back home with me.

Our end came after another drama. My spot got very hot, we were worried about the police, so I send her underground for a while. But the guy I send her to steals her stash and tries to force her to stay with him. She called me to let me know. I went to his place with 5 armed gang members. When we left the 3 guys that were there had to be hospitalized. We trashed the place so bad it looked like a tornado had been through there.

Like I said. Drama. Drama and fighting and violence.

Ironically enough, the night I met my future wife, I stabbed a guy twice in the chest. You know why? He owed me 50 bucks, that why!

Galatians 6

Whatever a man sows, he will reap in return

17:
Good Times

Up to this point I had always lived in a state of paranoia. It was not only the thought of getting bust by the police. Every spot I went to had its own set of rules and its own hierarchy. Mess with the rules or the hierarchy and you could end up dead. That's the way it ended for many.

Things in Cape Town were really intense. In the drug houses and locations, guys were losing their lives over a skew look or 2 bucks short change. Not to mention it was the time that a necklace became popular. A necklace is when a car tyre gets put over your head and squeezed around your body. A bit of petrol and a flame and that was the end of your life. Not a welcoming way to go. This was happening on a daily basis.

I lived in the midst of all of this. It was like life was in the balance by a breath. But I knew my place and I could handle myself if I had to. Having the right connections in that underworld was my biggest plus.

Then came the era of outdoor rave parties. It was like a dream. Operating with that much freedom. It was beyond believable. The location was always some piece of nature. The beach, a forest or up in the mountain. Huge tents were set up. There was music, food, fire and lots and lots of drugs.

I would send my runners out at the beginning of the evening, then they would come back around 1 am to restock. The thing is there were literally thousands of people. And everyone was on something.

The reason for the absolute freedom was that there was nothing the cops could do. They could not come in and arrest thousands of people for being on a substance. We were left alone.

The greatest thing for me was that after 2 am I would just take whatever I wanted and just join the party.

Of course, the other great advantage to these outdoor rave parties was that they went on for three days. It was never just one night. Big bucks, big freedom and a super cool party for myself. I also got to travel all over the country. The parties took place all along the coast at the most beautiful destinations.

I always needed at least a week to recover from one of these. Three days of drugs and no sleep is a lot for a man's body. And I was going to every single rave. Not just one every now and then.

Ecclesiastes 3

To everything, there is a season

18:
The End of That

"Man I think we should stash our gear before we go in there. You never know, let's play it safe." I was talking to Charles. I had around 50g of coke on me. We were about to go and score some other recreationals for the evening. I was worried that if they found out what I had on me, they would be more interested in taking mine than selling theirs.

"Good thinking," Charles responded, "let's find a safe spot to stash it."

We stop the car and I hide the coke in a secluded spot. We go score the pills we need for the evening and come back to get the coke. But the coke is not there.

"It's not here man!" I call out to Charles who I still sitting in the car. I look around. I see what looks like an abandoned building. But there is a security guard in front of it. I walk over to him.

"Did you see anyone here, did you take our sh*t?" I asked aggressively.

He tells me he doesn't know what I am talking about. But I know right off that he is lying. Charles call me back to the car.

"Here, give him 500 bucks and tell him to give the stuff back," he says.

"I think we should just split," I say "I haven't got a good feeling."

Charles was getting impatient with me "Just give him the money ok!"

"If you are sure man," I answered. I really didn't have a good feeling. Something was amiss.

But the guard would not take the money. He kept telling me he didn't know what I was talking about. I went back to the car.

"Look, Charles," I said "let's just go. I'll pay for the lost coke, but I want to go now."

Charles didn't like not getting his own way! And he was not about to take no for an answer. He insisted that I go back. I could feel myself getting angry. I felt like slamming him right in his twat face. I got out of the car again. By this time the security guard had returned to his spot in front of the building.

I stash the stuff we just bought.

I start off towards him again but I'm really angry. It's not worth the 50 grams. That's like half a night's earnings.

The next thing I know 6 police cars come screeching into the area. I knew it! I knew it! The first thought that goes through my head is

'Busted!'

Ecclesiastes 3

...a time to keep silent and a time to speak...

19: Busted

We spent the night in the holding cell. A few other guys shared our government lodgings for the night. They recognised us immediately so I knew there would be no trouble. But big mouth Charles was way out of his comfort zone. Between the withdrawal symptoms and the fear, he looked like a pasty-faced ghost. Had I not been there, I reckon those guys may have been tempted to have a little fun with him. Just a little mind you, he was still Charles after all.

In the morning his girlfriend baled us out. We drove straight back to the spot I stashed the pills and fetched them. The very spot we were busted. We proceeded to get very high. What a stressful night that was.

Between the haze of the buttons, we decided that I would take the rap. Charles had too many priors. He would do hard time. My statement was that poor Charles had no idea I was loaded with drugs when I got into his car.

Charles paid for the lawyer. He was cool. We did a few lines of coke the first time I met him. There were no nerves or stress. It was my first offence. I would get a suspended sentence and a fine.

After the sentencing, the problems came. I got 5 years suspended with a ten grand fine, the trouble was that I was very naïve.

You see Charles said if I took the rap it would not affect my job. He promised that I could continue to work for him. He lied straight to my face and there was not a single thing I could do about it.

There were two problems. Number one, I was in the system and the cops knew me. Number 2, by association, anyone who worked for me was also hot.

I was in a real predicament. The first thing anyone would think is, okay just go get a normal job. But the problem with that is I could never support my habit on a normal income. And I was nowhere near ready to quit drugs.

If I got caught with any significant amount of drugs on me, that would mean hard time for me.

Charles said I should get away for a while. He gave me some cash and told me to have a break. The cash was not enough. So I proceeded to rob some faceless person of 30 grand. That should hold me for a while.

I buggered off to a quiet town up on the coast.

Ecclesiastes 3

...a time to build up and a time to break down...

20:
Even Deeper

I laid low for a while and then I ran out of money and got really bored. I decided to head back to the mother city. I went to a friend's place. Avoided Charles. I understood that he wanted me out of his way. I took the rap so he would go free. But now I was persona non grata.

One night I was out messing around with some friends when someone offered me a hit on a little glass pipe.

Crack is the crystal form of cocaine. It comes in solid blocks or crystals which vary in colour, from pale yellow or rose to white. It is heated and then smoked. It derived its name because of the crackling sound it makes when heated. Crack is the most potent form of cocaine. It ranges from 75 to 100% pure.

Smoking Crack allows it to reach the brain more quickly and brings an intense and immediate high that is very short lived. The effects take 8 seconds to reach the brain. It releases a large amount of dopamine into the brain which induces a feeling of euphoria. The moment the dopamine level plummets there is an intense desire to do more.

The little glass pipe was too hot and I barely got a hit. But that messed up hit was enough. You have to remember that my first love, my true romance was always buttons. Buttons make you fall off the edge somewhere. This stuff shot you up further than the moon, right into the twilight zone. There was no comparison and I was hooked right from the very first messed up hit.

I recall a man once said to me '...never try that stuff, one is too many and 100 is not enough...'

I should have listened.

I still had all my connections at the drug houses and locations. I headed straight there. I wanted more of this crack. A lot more. I bought and smoked and bought and smoked and bought and smoked. It was just crazy. I was so hooked it was all I could do not to rob my own mother to get more.

I remember one night being out on the town. I checked out some of the old spots. I was on a downer since my high had worn off. I was always short of cash and I happened to see a guy who owed me a bit. I confronted him. He tried to blow me off, next thing I knew I had stabbed him twice in the chest. Then I kicked his head in and took his leather jacket. I mean he only owed me 50 bucks, but it made me feel better for a moment.

At one of the spots, I saw a Goddess at the door. I couldn't believe how incredibly beautiful she was. She took my breath away. The sight of her actually made me forget the downer I was on. I walked up to her and said 'I'm gonna marry you.'

Turns out she liked crack just as much as I did. Her name was Honey. It suited her too. Her skin was like liquid honey and she was just as sweet. We started hanging out. Hanging out in all the seedy places. Once we watched a woman give her body to a man for one hit on a pipe. The stuff was evil.

I slipped down that evil slide very fast. I was no longer in a position to afford my habit, so I took to robbing people. It was a dark time. Chasing the feeling that first hit gave me. It was elusive, I was chasing bad dreams and shadows. Word got out that I was now plain old bad news. I was not welcome anywhere. I spent all my time at Honey's place or the locations and crack houses.

She was hustling and shaking just as much as I was. We were both so hooked. We got to the point where it just felt like there was no one to hustle or scam or rob anymore. It felt like she was going and I was coming. She was Arthur and I was Mather. We were either too high or too strung out to realize the risks we were taking. We were literally at the end of the road. And it was a cul-de-sac.

Honey's family lived in Israel. We decided it was time for them to meet their future son in law.

Psalm 18

...you gave a wide place for my steps under me...

21:

Ready to Leave

We got the aeroplane tickets with any money we could beg, borrow or steal. Of course, we still had to get to Johannesburg. That's where the flight was leaving from. That was roughly 1200 km away. A 12-hour drive.

We hitchhiked there, smoking crack and buttons all the way. Once we got to the airport we threw every drug-related paraphernalia we had on us away.

12 Hundred kilometres of getting high and now a 12-hour flight to come down. It was a nightmare. Withdrawal from crack sets in quickly but ironically enough this was not what I was fighting. Withdrawals from buttons is worse. It literally makes you sick.

After the twin towers flying became a much more serious business. If I were to sit on a plane looking like that today, there is no doubt in my mind an air marshal would have arrested me.

I was shaking and sweating. I wanted to vomit. I had to control the urge the entire time. I knew how rough and heavy I was feeling. Fighting this war inside just willing myself to get through it and get to Israel. I looked over at Honey. Yeah, she was in the same nightmare. That was a very long 12 hours!

Her brother picked us up from the airport. We asked him to stop at the nearest store and we got a bottle of Vodka. That helped a lot. Once we were back at his place he made us a pipe. It was just weed, but it helped so much. We were in such bad shape after that flight.

For the next few days, I slept. Deep, much needed, comatose sleep. After that, it was time to meet her parents.

They were Jewish, religious and well set in their ways. They were not impressed that I wasn't. It took a lot of effort on my part, but eventually, they accepted me.

Jerusalem itself is either concrete jungle or dry barren stretches of land. I noticed that people spoke loudly. I don't know if it was just me, but it seemed like people spoke louder than in Cape Town. Almost like they were angry even if they weren't. Other than that it was a pretty chilled place to live. Not a lot of action. Which was nice for me, coming from so much action.

Honey's family were an interesting bunch. She had a couple of uncles which were in the Israeli taxi mafia. (Basically, a taxi service that has no competition. All competition is forced out. Tourists have to pay their ridiculously high prices since there is no alternative.)

She also had two cousins who were drug dealers. My kind of people and it didn't take me long to get my fingers dirty once again.

Isaiah 4

...for Jerusalem is ruined...because of their deeds...

22:
Jerusalem

Naturally, we end up moving in with one of her cousins. It was par for the course. Living with a dealer. This was my comfort zone. Let's call him Shay.

Shay was small time. Weed, ecstasy and coke were his business. People constantly popping in and out of his spot. Score, leave. Score, leave.

I gave everything I had in patience to cook up his coke and make my precious crack. But the coke was so cut and diluted it was impossible to even get a tiny rock out of it. In the end, I gave up trying. I had to satisfy my appetite with E and weed and tons of booze.

Needless to say, Shay was pretty impressed with my streetwise. I wasn't small time. Before long I was his top dog. I may have changed countries but that was all. It was literally a matter of same sh*t different country. And things got heavy there too.

I mean, I didn't even stop to think about the depth of that. I left South Africa. I came to Israel, which is actually one of the spiritual meccas of the world. And I packed every bit of baggage from my whole life. Everything I had carried. All the hurt. All the pain. All the fear. All the hate. I left nothing behind. Meticulously, I packed those bags and dragged them all the way to Israel!

One day Shay comes to me and tell me he has a bit of a problem and needs my help to fix it. It turns out some guys owe him money and are not coughing up. He needs me to get heavy with them. But he doesn't leave the heavy up to me. He has his own plan. But I am the one who has to execute it.

I get in the taxi and tell him where I want him to go. He does what he is told and pulls up to the curb.

"Wait here," I tell him "I'll be back in a few minutes."

I walk around the corner out of his line of sight. My mind is racing. 'this is a stupid idea, David, what the hell are you doing? What the hell are you thinking? Are you actually going to go through with this?'

I spot my target. It's a car. I walk up to it and smash the window. Reach my hand in and empty the gasoline bottle in my hand.

My mind again.

'What if I catch fire? What if there is gasoline on my hand and the flame leaps on to me?'

I drop a match into the car and quickly step back.

Wooooooof

It was instant. I thought I may have to wait a bit. I admire my handiwork for a moment. Then I feel the rush. Almost like hitting something good.

I hightail back to the waiting taxi. Jump in.

"Yalla, Yalla," I shout at him. That Arabic for, Go! Go!

In the back of the taxi, the rush settles down a bit. I got away. I didn't get caught! Wheew!

What you have to understand is that an act like this gives a man a really good street rep. This is the reason I did things like this. So everyone would know, don't mess with David. Or the sh*t will get serious.

The next day I did the same thing to remind another of his debt. I got paid in drugs. Which was fine with me. It's what I would use the money for anyway. But the biggest payment was what it said about me.

We messed around in Jerusalem for a few more months. It was good times. I felt like a big fish in a small pond. But after a while, we got itchy feet again. Honey suggested that we move to Tel Aviv. She had another cousin there and it had a lot more going on. So we moved to Tel Aviv.

Psalm 7

...and he is angry with the wicked every day...

23: Tel Aviv

Tel Aviv is known as the party capital of the Middle East. Located on the Mediterranean coastline, it is Israel's largest metropolitan area. It is home to many foreign embassies and is ranked as one of the global financial centres of the world. It receives over 2.5 million international visitors every year. It has the largest university in the country which is home to some 30 000 students.

I felt like I had arrived in New York. What a place. We moved in with Honey's cousin and her boyfriend. He was an amazing guy. Very peaceful. Which was a huge contrast to everyone that I had known or was close to.

I mellowed out a lot myself. I got a job at a factory. My Hebrew was improving daily. I was diligent about learning the language and it paid off.

I enjoyed working in the factory. There is such a vast difference between taking drugs and selling drugs. As opposed to taking drugs and not selling drugs.

Dealing means that even when you are high and just want to chill, you are still hustling and missioning. Constant action. Don't get me wrong, I still sold a bit of weed for extra cash. But that was so small it was like nothing.

Hamish, the cousin's boyfriend, was something of a guru to the people. He had something about him that drew people in. They wanted to be around him.

When we moved and got a new and bigger place together, I watched people come over and bring him weed and hash. I swear that guy never paid for a single thing.

He took us to trance parties. They were nothing like what we were used to in South Africa. South African trance parties were about how smashed everyone could get.

You must remember that Israel is a war-ridden country. People live under a serious amount of stress. These parties were like an escape for them. Sure, everyone got smashed, but it was a different headspace. And I really enjoyed it.

We'd been there for a few months when Hamish told us that he and his girlfriend were going to India for a few months. This was bliss for Honey and I. We never had real alone time. I loved Tel Aviv and I loved the peace it brought out in me. I felt home. Home and safe.

But when they got back from India they wanted to get married and have a family. There was no longer space for Honey and I.

We decided to go back to Cape Town. We'd been out of the scene for a year and a half. We didn't think anyone would mind or care if we returned.

1 Corinthians 10

Let no one seek his own good, but the good of his neighbour.

24:
Cleaning Up

It was pretty great to be back. Home is home. My parents had really missed me and were very happy to see me again. Honey and I moved in with them. A temporary plan until I got a job.

I wanted a job. A real job. You see, by my standards, I was almost clean. I mean I smoked weed and drank. Maybe do the occasional recreational. But nothing like I was before Israel. I didn't feel demon-driven to get my next high. Like I said, by my standards I was clean.

I looked for a job for a while. But it was harder than you'd think. I had never actually worked in Cape Town. I had no idea what kind of job to look for. I couldn't see myself packing shelves in a supermarket. I also couldn't see myself as a sales rep for some arbitrary product.

The phrase beggars can't be choosers comes to mind. But it wasn't like that. If I was going to start a new life then I wanted it to be with something that suited me, something that I could actually enjoy.

This straight thing wasn't so easy. I remember thinking that leaving Israel was a bad idea. We should have tried somehow. Got better jobs, got out own spot.

Old friends heard that I was back in town. They started visiting at my mom's house. I use the term friends loosely. Who I was before I went to Israel, well I didn't really have friends. I had people. Because the greeting went something like this. 'Hey bro, good to have you back man, you were missed. So what's up? Can you organise some sh*t for us?'

That was it, they were all just popping by to see if I could score for them. I was the one who had the balls and the connections to go to the locations and the drug houses. It's 'not like anyone could just stroll in there and score.

But I was firm, kept saying no, I'm done with all that. People were surprised. Some didn't believe me. Kept asking even after I said no.

One day a guy comes over and tells me he is having a house party. Nothing heavy. Just some weed and some booze. I wanted to go. I had been hanging at my mother's house too long. I needed an out. Honey and I discussed it. We said that if he was lying and there was heavy sh*t there. We would just leave. We were both proud of our newly found relative sobriety.

Genesis 13

Now the men of Sodom were wicked...

25: House Party

My mind, 'David you can't stay at this party, you have to leave right now!! Okay, that would look strange. Like a pussy. Okay, one beer and then you are so out of here.'

You name it and it was happening in this house. I'm serious. Name it!

Alcohol? Yes.

Weed? Yes.

Coke? Yes.

Ecstacy? Yes.

Speed? Yes.

Sex? Yes.

It was like Sodom and Gomorrah. I stayed in the kitchen, trying to have my beer without looking at all the temptations.

A random person starts talking to me. "So have you heard? Charles is small time now. Got pushed out by a stronger power."

The guy was on speed, I could see his jaw clenching while he was speaking.

"This power runs security on every single nightclub now man. No one would ever mess with him. Even his own men get killed."

The speed was obviously giving this guy a loose tongue. But it was good to know. Charles was out. In some deep way that made me feel really good. The guy burned me, man. After what I did for him. Loyalty is everything. If he had only had my back, I would have still had his.

This information made old wounds surface. I don't like old wounds. And the smell in there. What was up with my nose? I could smell each drug. The chemical smell of coke was wafting in my nostrils. I could actually taste it.

Fu*k it!

I did a line. Then two more.

Honey didn't need much persuading. It was kind of like, twist my rubber arm.

We stayed until the sun was high in the sky the next day. And I was just as high as the sun when I went home.

I could tell by my mother's face that she knew.

Another friend came around later that afternoon. Made me a button. That sweet familiar smell.

I fell off the end in the thunderclouds. I was with Hamish at a trans party. My mother was staring at me. Angry eyes. Disappointed eyes. I came back.

"Tell Hamish to come and have a hit man," I said to no one in particular.

"Who's Hamish?" No one answered.

"Never mind," I smiled.

That was all it took. I was hook, line and sinker. Back on the buttons. They were my weakness. I was not kidding when I called them my first love. My true romance. You always have a weak spot for that special one. When she comes knocking, you just have to open the door.

Two days after that button I was back on crack too.

I needed a plan. I had to get out of my parent's house. Needed my own spot. Needed privacy to court my love. Needed money, a lot of it. It was time to hustle. The hustler was back in town!

Isaiah 34

...the night monster will settle there...

26:
The Hustler

Just like that, I had a job! When I was trying to stay straight I just couldn't find a job. Now that the motivation was there, well it was no problem. I found the perfect job. I became a barman.

I had nothing to do with the new power in town. I just sold the drinks. The door belonged to the power. Of course, we both know I didn't only sell drinks. I sold anything you wanted. And business was booming.

I was in a better position than before Israel. Here I had a cover job. I wasn't anyone's top dog. I was my own dog. I liked that. Sure I had to re-visit old connections. Those connections were still strong and they were happy to see my face. I was good business. Good, fast money.

I'm a quick study and before long I got promoted. To bar manager. That suited me just fine. I had my own guys work at the bar counter. They were now delivering the goods to the thirsty patrons.

I got a townhouse in the area behind the bar. It was perfect. The neighbouring houses were mostly empty and there was tons of empty space all around. I'd throw huge parties there. I'd stock up with booze I helped myself to at the bar. After all, I was a manager and I had the keys.

The general manager did know what I was up to. But he never said a word. He knew exactly who my new best friend was and he was terrified of him. Fear was that man's enemy. He eventually blew his own brains out for fear that someone would beat him to it.

My new best friend was Botha. Well, he wasn't really my best friend, but he was always around me. He ran a hardcore gang and he had the war marks to prove his commitment.

He'd been shot a few times, had bullet wounds too. I think he like coming to my place because it was an escape from all the action in the ganglands.

The only problem was that this man was not small time. He moved anything and everything. He had a sweet spot for cars though. Sometimes there would be as many as three hot cars in my garage at my house! But you learn to live with that kind of thing.

But I was in deeper than my comfort zone. I didn't enjoy driving around with a bulletproof vest to protect myself. I was paranoid all the time. Worse than ever before. New gangs were forming all the time. Ironically enough, the worst of them was the gang that promised to take out all the gangs. Imagine that? A gang to stop gangs? And the people swallowed it. They were well supported.

It was at this point that I decided to settle an old score. I went to see the backstabber, Charles. He was running women. How low can you go? I was disgusted. But I plastered a friendly smile on my face and asked him for 20 caps of acid. Said I would bring the cash the next day. I could tell he was weary of me but my plastered smile won him over. He gave me the caps. And I returned the next day. His smile was genuine. Maybe he thought I could bring him back in the game. He couldn't actually sell. The gangs would take him out.

He knew I still had my gang connections. I asked for a bit more and he gave it. I came back a few days later with the cash. Then I asked for a big number. I saw the split second hesitation in his eyes. But he gave it to me. Idiot!

A few days later he calls me and says he wants the cash. I tell him I'm in no condition to drive but he can come and collect it. He gets to my spot and sees Botha. The blood literally drains from his face.

"The cash is inside on the table," I say.

He hesitates. Looks at Botha again and leaves.

Score settled.

Neither of us cared about the money or the acid. Charles just got his

Sit! Stay! Roll over! Good boy!

Ephesians 5

...do not be partakers with them, for you were formerly darkness...

27:
Sonny

One night I had been out on a mission, I went back to the bar to make sure everyone was doing their job. I go up the stairs to the bar and I see a black guy has been dragged on to my countertop. And a huge white guy is laying into him.

I don't think so, not in my bar.

Calmly I walked behind the counter. Removed a big fat Sambuca bottle and proceeded to smash it right in the white guy's face.

Lots of blood.

Screaming... that was his girlfriend.

The black guy and I smile at each other and then kick the white guy's ugly bleeding face in.

I'm white, and I got no time for racists.

The Sambuca bottle is black. Blue Sambuca and red blood.

Turns out, the black guy is actually Indian. His name is Sonny. We get talking and I realize he has no prospects in life. Dead end job. Nothing happening. So I offer him a job. I like him. That's rare for me.

I like him because he is just like me. He is a little younger and a little blacker. But me. He didn't even know it. But I did. And I was going to hook him up. Introduce him to the underground, that's where he would shine.

So I set Sonny up. He is a natural. He is hustling and shaking like an old pro. Sometimes a person just knows these things.

I remember being at home in my garage. I'd just hit a button. I was actually leaning up against a stolen car. I was busy falling off the edge when I heard a voice. The voice carried a smile.

"Don't I know you from somewhere?" I rushed into the smile. Lingered there for a while. Then rushed out again.

I think that was the moment our friendship was sealed. The person behind that voice was warm and extremely loyal. A quality I value so highly.

Sonny had never smoked buttons before. We changed that. As we floated in and out of each other's minds I realized that this guy was different. That our connection would be lifelong.

"Hey Sonny, you want to seal it?" I asked him.

He looked at me confused.

"With blood," I said "brothers for life."

Sonny smiled. I reached for a blade. My wife started freaking out.

"Don't be stupid Gerry! You can get aids man!"

Sonny's girlfriend said the same thing. Sonny actually got an aids test after that night. At his girlfriend's insistence of course.

The truth is, with or without the spilling and sharing of blood, Sonny and I were always connected.

1 Corinthians 15

Do not be deceived: 'Bad company corrupts good morals.'

28:
David and Sonny

Sonny and I had some crazy times. I'm just going to share them randomly. Because to be honest we were always so sh*t faced I can't remember the order in which things happened.

We were always running out of money, which is crazy because we earned a lot of it. But our habit was up to 2 grand a day. Who can keep up with that right? I remember one time we were already really high. We wanted more but had no money.

"Let's rob a predator," Sonny suggests. "A paedophile fag."

He is smiling and I join in. I like that idea. Robbing a corrupt person doesn't leave a bad taste in my mouth. So I dress in some jeans and a tight white t-shirt.

We drive to a popular spot and I go and stand under a streetlight. Didn't take long. An old man pulls up in his Mercedes Benz. I get in the car and stick a pen in his neck. Only took a few seconds. Grab his wallet and hightail back to Sonny's car.

We speed off and just a few metres down the road Sonny's car runs out of gas. How ridiculous is that? We jump out of the car and run. It sounds like something from a crazy movie, but I kid you not. Every word is true!

Sonny's car is a story unto itself. The windscreen was shattered. There were bits and pieces missing yet somehow it was still holding itself together. It was old, rusty and always on empty. And yet for some reason we always used it. The one time he actually took it to a mechanic I lent him one of my cars. One of my stolen cars. A little later that day I'm just chilling and pottering around at home and I hear this screeching of tyres.

Sonny jumps out of the car. He looks white. It turns out he crashed into another car but fled the scene. Obviously not wanting to be caught in a stolen car. We had to dump that car that night.

I took Sonny to his first outdoor rave party. I was looking forward to it because I knew that he would really enjoy it. His plan was to sell a few recreational for the first part of the evening and then join the party. But the organisers of the rave take his stash. I get wind of this and let them know in no uncertain terms that if they do not return it, I would unleash hell on their little rave. They politely complied.

Another time we decided to head to the city for a night on the town. Sonny is off his face on ecstasy, so I drive. We both have sunglasses on since little bits of windscreen keep flying off into our faces. All of a sudden it starts raining. Now the windscreen is so badly damaged that the wipers don't work. Sonny's seatbelt also doesn't work. I can't see a thing yet I clearly remember unclipping my seat belt. 'If he dies I die.'

This was the extent of our bond.

Proverbs 28

The wicked man runs away...

29:
Checking Out

"David, we need to talk." Honey was addressing me. I hated it when she said that. Any time she said 'we need to talk' it was always something serious. I had to pay attention. Trouble is I was always so high I struggled to pay attention.

"What's up?" I asked.

"Botha is tied up in court all the time with that gun smuggling thing. This house is going to the dogs. No one has any respect when he is not around. Trouble is coming, I'm telling you. Big trouble. And I want no part of it."

She was right. Botha commanded respect. I could if I wanted to. But all I wanted was my buttons and my crack. People were just coming and going any time night and day. We were living in a good neighbourhood. At some point, someone was going to call the cops.

"You are right," I said.

"And David you are so thin, you have to take it easy yourself. Take a timeout, you know," she continued. She had concern in her voice. She still used too, but nothing like I did.

"What would I do without you? If the cops come here I would lose you. This place has so many drugs, stolen goods and lawbreakers. They would take you away. I can't handle that."

What can I say? She was right again. I would do hard time if this place got busted.

"So what do you want to do babe?" I asked her.

She came over and put her arms around me.

"Let's go and visit Hamish." She kisses me.

My head becomes very busy. It's not a bad idea. But we can't tell anyone about it. We will have to say we are taking a weekend away for some down time together.

There would be a meltdown if these guys thought I was baling on them.

My mind went to Sonny. I really didn't want to leave him out of the loop.

Money! We would need quite a bit of it.

I would do the projector scam. That was quick bucks. I'd sent pretty girls to go and rent projectors. I'd give them fake I.D.s they would say the needed them for an outdoor rave. For the big white screen. They earned a grand for ten minutes work. I would the sell the projectors for 15 grand a pop.

In the end, I told Sonny. There was no way I could leave without saying goodbye. He was very pissed off with me.

Luke 4

And he led him to Jerusalem...

30: Back

We went back to Jerusalem. We had quite a lot of money from the projector scam so we got our own place straight away. No staying with family this time.

The kind of substance I was abusing my body with was not available here. I was feeling so rough from the flight and withdrawal symptoms. I remember taking a shower and afterwards just standing in front of the mirror looking at my naked body.

I was shocked. I was literally skin and bone. Looked like a prisoner of war victim. I couldn't believe that I never noticed how thin I was. I didn't even notice that my clothes must have been hanging on me. I really needed to clean up my act.

When I looked in that mirror I saw someone that was on death's door.

It took two weeks of hell. Two weeks of sweating and vomiting and trembling. It was the worst withdrawal I had ever been through. But I did it.

After it was over I told Honey that I was going straight. Get a real job. No more hustling. No more hectic abuse of my body. I still drank and smoked weed. But that was it.

I was looking for a job and then I ran into some luck, I met a fellow South African. His name was Richard and he just happened to have his own business. He told me it was hard work. So I had to be sure I wanted a job with him. He owned a renovation company. He was not kidding about the hard work. The first day I actually vomited from the stress of it. He had me work a jackhammer on his patio. My body was still jolting way into the night.

But it was good for me. It was hard and honest work. I felt like I was being punished and I wanted it. Got to a point where I could go for eight hours straight. I could feel that my body was strong again. I liked the new man in the mirror.

Richard was Jewish, religiously so. You know how some people belong to a religion, but they don't actually practise it. Well, he was not like that. He took me to places outside of the city. High up in the hills where we could look down at the vast culture and tradition Jerusalem held.

We spoke of Jesus and the idea of whether He was a prophet or the Messiah.

I really started to think about that. I mean I was no religious person. But I started going off by myself. Finding places to sit and ponder. If Jesus was real, then He walked here. That was a pretty crazy idea. Walking the same streets that Jesus did. Whether you believe in him or not, it's still historically profound. In a huge way!

The sounds of the prayers being sung echoed through the entire city. It made me feel peaceful inside. The last time I was here I barely noticed it.

I had a tiny Bible in my backpack and for some reason, I started reading it. I enjoyed reading it. In many ways, the Bible is like a big self-help book. Lots of what is written there makes sense and if you apply it to your life, really does change things. Just something as simple as not getting angry with an angry person. Be kind to an angry person. That will end their anger. It's simple and true.

Life was good for a change. And then Honey fell pregnant.

Proverbs 14

He faithless in heart will be filled with his own ways...

31:
A Second Job

I was excited. I was going to be a dad. What a crazy idea. I had tons of mixed feelings but the winner was excitement. Honey had to stop working. So we didn't have enough money. And we would need even more when the little one came along. I realized I would need to get a second job for a while.

I asked around and eventually, one of the neighbours said her son ran a bar and could use some help.

A bar. Did I say a bar? The place was the biggest nightclub I have ever seen. It looked like it used to be a warehouse. There were five bars. Some of the best trance DJ'S. Music, dancing, the pace was always packed.

I worked there on the weekends and kept my renovation job during the week. Tips were good, money was good. We were doing okay. And I loved the job. It was an excuse to party on the weekends.

One night...

"Hey, Dave, you have been here a while now. It's time you took one of these and really worked that bar."

I looked down at the 'E' lying in the palm of her hand.

One wouldn't do anything. It's not like it's a button or crack.

I just blinked. That's how it was. In one blink I was hustling again. Running the entire show.

Pushing ecstasy over the counter. Stealing from the register. Guys were giving me recreationals in the street just to get into that club. It was always full. Not everyone got in.

Next thing you know the manager leaves. Who gets his job `Yup! I did. Been there done that got the t-shirt. I had the keys to everything. I had veto on the door. Everyone wanted to make me happy just for a bit of the action.

Of course, my relationship with Honey barely existed anymore. And my daughter was a smile on my face for the few moments I spent with her when I had time. All that connected Honey and I were the drugs. We were either on them or hanging for them.

Now we had a daughter to connect us, but my mind was in that club. Not on my family.

Like I said, people were constantly giving me recreationals. One kid shows up and gives me about 100g of heroin. Turns out he stole it from some dealer and doesn't actually know what to do with it. Go figure!

I chased the dragon. But I never caught her. But the idea of her was warm, so very warm. And nothing could touch it. It was like being back in the womb, warm comforted and safe.

I chased for about eight months. Lost all the weight I gained. Lost my new found strength. Lost many days at work. Lost my mind for a while. And finally almost lost my daughter.

Honey put her foot down. Dragon or daughter.

Once again I found myself cleaning up.

Proverbs 31

...and remember their misery no more...

32:
Brief South African Visit

So I was clean again. Getting clean was starting to feel like those fake nails Honey was always sticking on her fingertips. On again, off again, on again, off again.

In life sometimes we are up, and sometimes we are down. I was once again in an up time. Peaceful. I no longer worked at the club. Honey's family was helping out where we needed. Then my parents let me know that my Grandmother had died and I was to come home for her funeral.

They were happy to see me. It was obvious I was clean and healthy. We went to my gran's funeral and when I left the funeral I went straight to my old connections and got some buttons. Just like that!

It's a crazy thing and it's hard to explain. But the temptation was just too great. My precious buttons weren't available in Israel. But they were here. How could I possibly miss that opportunity?

I figured I'd just clean up again when I went back. I was getting good at it by now.

Fake nails...

It was Wednesday and my flight was only on Monday. So I had a few precious days to enjoy my illicit affair. I popped into my old bar, had a few drinks with the new manager. By

Friday I had the crack going too. My last weekend with my love.

Then my phone rings. It's Botha and he wants me to fetch him.

WHAT? How does he even know that I am in town? UGH! I should never have gone to the bar! Big mouth manager!

Trouble is, Botha got hard time for that gun smuggling sh*t. He had just escaped prison. He was literally a fleeing felon. What was I going to do? I couldn't say no. So I went. Buttoned up, cracked up, fetching an escaped felon. Not good man.

The first thing he wants is crack. So I take him to score and we hit the glass pipe. Then he wants to see his wife. WHAT? That's the first place the cops are going to look. He is adamant. Wants to see his wife.

The plan is to drop him at a safe house. Then I would fetch his wife and bring her to his location. But when I approached the pickup spot for his wife I knew the cops were on her. I hightailed out of there. Now what? They definitely saw my car.

I go and wake Sonny up. I take a 5 litre can of petrol with me. Sonny never has petrol in his car. We go back to find Botha. But he is not there. This whole mission is such a mess! After driving around for a while I think, well fu*k it! I'll go home. Lie low till Monday and just get the hell out of here.

I drive around my own block a few times, checking that it's safe. Looks good. By now it's six in the morning and all I want to do is fall into bed and sleep. What a heavy night that was.

I walk in the door and my dad is sitting in the living room with two cops from the gang and gun unit.

"Where is he?" They ask.

"Dunno," I say.

"Tell us or you are coming with us." They say.

"Let's go," I say.

There goes my Monday flight. Who knows how long these guys are going to keep me. They take me down to the station and question me some more. My answer stays the same. I get thrown into a cell.

Idiots were so worried about where Botha was they forgot to search me. I pull the pipe out of my shoe and take a few good hits. Float out of that cell.

A little later I float back in and they come back in. Tell me I am free to go on the condition that I leave the country today.

Blink, blink and I'm on a flight back to Israel.

Matthew 18

If a man has 100 sheep and one of them goes astray, does he not leave the 99 on the mountain and go and search for the one...

33:
Sonny's story

So here I was back in Israel detoxing again. I started to think about Sonny. I pitched up at his house in the middle of the night after not seeing him for years. He didn't ask any questions. Just helped. There aren't too many of those around.

Here's the crazy thing. He comes from a good home. His uncle is a pastor and his parents are missionaries. Travelling the country, spreading the good news.

I tried to remember the conversation we had when we were driving around looking for Botha. He was working security for the Power now. He said they saw him in a fight and they offered him a job. A job that he was so good at, he got promoted to manager.

"So what does management do Bro?" I asked him.

He laughs. That's another thing I value about him. He always finds a reason to laugh.

"I got promoted to the position of a cleaning lady." He laughs again.

I knew all about that. Management. One car 4 guys strong. Deliver and collect whatever needs delivering or collecting. But the main issue was trouble in the clubs. Trouble that got out of control. Management would be called. Five cars arrive. Each 4 guys strong. Trouble ended quickly. Cleaning up.

I was worried about Sonny. I didn't like him working for the Power. There was no loyalty there. If Sonny missed a beat he could end up dead. Not to mention that ridiculous group that claims to be fighting gangs. They are the worst gang of all. And everyone knows the target the Power.

Sonny is speaking again, "Man I'm on tik if the Power finds out I'm dead."

Tik is the South African street name for crystal methamphetamine. Its effects are stronger and last longer than other forms of meth, but the crash is also much worse.

The high is euphoric, energetic, confident and secure.

The crash is sweaty aggression with headaches and panic.

"The Power wanted to send me to Joburg. I donered (beat up) the wrong guy. But David, something crazy is going on. I tried to go. I got in my car and it just won't go faster than 80kmph. I tried three days in a row. Something bad is gonna happen in Joberg. I'm sure that's why the car won't go."

It was my turn to laugh. "That car never goes."

"I'm serious man. Anyway, I'm going on a trip with some missionaries to Mozambique," he said.

"You going where?" I thought I heard him wrong.

"I don't care about their purpose; I just need to get away. The power has bad plans for me and he doesn't even know I'm on tik."

So Sonny was going to Mozambique. Good for him. I never trusted the Power. I'm glad he was getting away from that.

Romans 3

No one is righteous
Not even one
No one is truly wise
No one is seeking God
All have turned away
All have become useless
No one does good
Not a single one
Their talk is foul, like the stench from an open grave
Their tongues are filled with lies
Snake venom drips from their lips
Their mouths are full of cursing and bitterness
They rush to commit murder
Destruction and misery always follow them
They don't know where to find peace

They have no fear of God at all

34: Grace

I chilled and did the family thing in Israel. I knew my visa needed to be renewed and I would have to fly back to South Africa to do that. After the last trip, I was not so keen to go.

On the plus side, I was going to hook up with Sonny who was back from his missions in Mozambique.

The next part is very predictable. I land in South Africa and go and score. It's who I am. Can't help myself. I go on a bender for a few days. I mean it's like when you have no money and you are starving. Then your luck changes and all of a sudden you have money. You don't go and buy an apple. You get 2 burgers, 2 portions of fries, 2 milkshakes and dessert.

Sonny calls me.

'I'm picking you up tomorrow Bro."

I'm thinking, cool Sonny, is coming to the bender.

He picks me up in the morning, same old car. Some things never change. But there is a girl in the car. She looks conservative. Weird.

I ask him where we are going. He mentions the area. Okay, drugs prostitution. Maybe she is a working girl. She doesn't look the type. But what do I know? I hit a pipe in the back of the car. Pass it to Sonny who declines. Weird…

We walk into an old movie house. Some homeless at the door. Prostitutes going in. Lots of junkies too. Familiar faces. I don't know what we are doing here. I assume Sonny has business.

Then the penny drops. It's a church. But I don't feel uncomfortable. I like it. It's chilled. All the people are chilled. Music is playing. But not church organ music. Good music.

I fell relaxed, it's almost inviting. A guy goes to the front and starts speaking. I figure he must be the pastor. Even though he is wearing jeans and a t-shirt.

I start listening to him. His words aren't washing over my head anymore. I am hearing them. They are penetrating my mind. Like a spear, it's penetrating...my mind...my heart...twisting...deeper and deeper...

An overwhelming sense of something came over me... shame...so much shame...guilt...sorrow...pain...disgust at myself...

I was so sorry...sorry...life is a gift...I treated it like dirt under my shoes...mine and others...

I belonged in hell...I saw all the witches and warlocks...all the evil people...in hell with me...we belonged there...

I started crying...crying for all the people I had hurt...crying for all the disgusting things I have done...crying for how much I had hurt myself...the depth of those tears are beyond words...heavy...heavy dark sorrow...

I did not know it at the time, but those were tears of repentance...

'Amazing grace, how sweet the sound, that saved a wretch like me...'

I am a wretch...that is me..

Then the love came. I felt myself move from complete and terrible darkness into the light...the beautiful forgiving light...I could feel Him speak...I forgive you...I already paid for you...I suffered for you...you don't have to suffer...let it go...I will take it from you...

The tears are flowing freely...now they are tears of joy...tears of freedom...tears of relief...

'I once was lost, but now I'm found...'

I was no longer lost...life has meaning...MY life has meaning...I am unconditionally loved and forgiven...

A young girl came up to me and took my hand...she led me to the front of the church and I gave my life to Jesus...

This is not a new chapter. I just wanted to leave the rest of the previous page open. Leave it to Jesus and all the things that were left unsaid.

Sonny was smiling at me.

What in the world made Sonny bring me here.

I could feel Jesus in his smile.

Dave and Sonny, the two worst junkie gangsters, standing smiling at each other in the presence of Jesus.

I want to take a moment to try and explain something. I know who I was. I have tried to be honest in telling this story. But a lot got left out. Only because if I tell about beating up a guy or stabbing a guy. You heard it. It's boring to read the same thing over and over again. But if I beat up a guy, I beat up hundreds. If I robbed one person, I robbed hundreds. The things I did, the person I was, disappeared that day.

When God shows up, it's supernatural. It's nothing like anything in this world. And there is no drug on the planet that can give you that peace or joy.

2 Thessalonians

It was for this He called you...

35: Mozambique

Sonny had gone with the missionaries to Mozambique to escape from the Power. He thought he would lay low for a while and return once things had cooled down. Little did he know that trip to Mozambique would change his life.

Initially, he was horrified at the poverty and the desperate circumstances of the people. But then he noticed that these people were happy. They lived with a sense of purpose. Each days work brought reward. Nobody was looking for any kind recreational escape.

Women and older children would get up in the morning and go to work in the fields for the farmers. Or they would go and set up street stalls with food or homemade crafts. These stalls were mostly supported by tourists. Men would also work on farms and street stalls and many of them built. They built mud houses.

Sonny met a teacher who had been saving all his life. He told Sonny that when he finally had enough money, he would buy a tin roof for his mud house. For some reason, this stuck with Sonny. This man's lifelong dream was a tin roof for his mud house.

What a strong contrast this was to the life Sonny knew. Fighting over play-stations and cell phones. Robbing people for money for drugs. That was the life that did not make sense. This life here in Mozambique did make sense.

He started to feel the peace of the people. He started to enjoy the way they lived.

One day Sonny helped them build a church. It was a hard day's work in the summer heat. That day Sonny felt the call on his heart. Silently he stood in front of that church and gave his life to the Lord.

He didn't talk about it or tell anyone about it. But the Holy Spirit moved in and Sonny changed that day.

When he returned to Cape Town, he went straight to the Power and told them the truth. Told them that he had given his life to the Lord. They let him go, just like that. It's an amazing thing having someone that powerful behind your back.

Sonny got a real job. He became a sales rep. He sold gold teeth to dental companies. He found that quite amusing since he was a black Indian man.

Psalm 31

...my life is in your hands...

36:
My Life is in Your Hands

When I got back to Israel everyone was happy. I mean, prior to this, every time I left I came back hooked on crack and buttons. I had to detox. It was a lot for my wife and child. Not this time. I didn't even smoke cigarettes anymore. Absolutely nothing. I was truly free. Not a single addiction on my body or my mind.

I loved being in Jerusalem. Jesus walked here. On the very streets walk! That just blew me away.

But there was a downside too. War had flared up again. We were living with tanks and guns and bombs. And it as getting worse by the day. I was also having trouble because none of these people believed that Jesus was the Messiah. I knew that He was! He is the son of God! He was in that church! He set me free! Because of this, I didn't have anywhere to take my questions.

For all the war going on around me, I was peaceful. I had a real routine. Something I never had before. I would get up early each day and spend some time with God. My bus to work was at 7.45 every morning. Bus number 32. I loved walking and talking to God. But I was still confused as to what I was supposed to do with my life now. What did God want me to do? And how was I supposed to know or find out what He wanted?

I guess there are people that know all about this stuff. People with answers to my questions. Maybe some people reading this think WTF now it's a Christian book??? But I don't see it that way. I don't have any time for religion. I mean I respect these people here in Israel. They have their traditions. But inside myself I just know that God is real, Jesus did something inside me. That something is what people need, not religious ideas. That isn't gonna do it.

The only thing I learned in the rest of my time in Israel, is that when you get on your knees and give your life to God, He looks after you.

I got up one morning, spent some time with Hm. Had breakfast and headed out the door to catch my bus to work. My phone rings.

"David, walk over to my house this morning. We need to go and look at some work in the industrial area."

That's a first I thought. Been catching that bus for three years. So I change direction and start walking to Richard's house. It was close enough. The next thing I know I'm taking cover. Massive explosion. It was close by. Then tons of black smoke, sirens, screaming.

A bus had been bombed. And yes. Later that day I found out it was the 7:45 am bus number 32!

The good Lord had a purpose for me! He could have taken me straight to heaven that day. My salvation was secured. But he didn't.

Somehow I knew that I had to go home. Back to South Africa. Make amends. Face my demons so to speak.

Isaiah 45

I will go before you and level the mountains...

37: Living

Going back to South Africa was complicated. I had never been able to stay clean in this country. Temptation was everywhere, and I succumbed to it every time. Now I was here to make amends.

When I packed my stuff in Israel, I packed 2 crack pipes. They had been improvised and improved upon in my time in Israel. I told myself there would serve as a reminder of the life I once led. But when I walked out of the airport I felt the pull of those pipes. The pull of temptation. I knew what I had to do.

I took them out of my bag and stood on them, right there at the airport. My mind was made up, I was not going down that road again. But it's like a raging war inside between forces of good and evil.

At first, we went to live with my parents. Of course, this was not ideal. My parents are quiet people who are set in their ways. I came with a wife and a three-year-old daughter. I needed a job yesterday. And we needed our own place to stay.

Here's the crazy thing, the Bible says that God will level mountains for us. And these were mountains to me. I never had a real job. Bar work is not a real job to me. I mean a 9 to 5 job. I'm not qualified to do anything either. But I get wind that an airline is looking for staff that can speak Hebrew.

Perfect. Now I got a job. What's more, I get promoted twice within months of working there.

I also need a place to stay. A place I can afford. I find a beautiful house right under the mountain. The owner decides she likes me. She doesn't ask for a deposit and charges me half the rent she is charging the neighbour. The houses are pretty much exactly the same.

I'm not kidding. When God puts His hand in your life things change. They really do. And please don't get me wrong. I'm no happy-clappy go to church guy who follows all their man-made rules. I'm just a guy living my life who has a relationship with his creator. I really think that is the way it's supposed to be. I guess there are some good churches. Fellowship is important. But I am not prepared to go to the 60 getting it wrong just to find the one getting it right. For now, I'm happy to just spend time with God and let Him lead me.

Sonny introduced me to some of his family who went into the locations and townships to preach the word of God. I asked them if I could join them. These were the very same places the younger me rode shirtless on his bike. The same places the older me got high. Now I was here to tell them about Jesus.

It was incredible! I spoke their language in more ways than one. I knew what was inside their heads. I had been there. I was able to reach people on their level and draw them to Jesus. I was confident and sure of myself, not because I was high, but because He was with me.

Isaiah 43

Behold I will do a new thing…

38: Leaving Again

Honey and I had another child. A second daughter. That is when I started to think about our life in South Africa. The Apartheid era had ended. This was something I was very happy about. I had never looked at colour, only ever at people. But unfortunately, reverse-racism was now alive and well.

White people were no longer getting employed. And it was not subtle. It was literally a matter of 'Sorry but we cannot interview you for the position because you are white.'

This did not affect me in a big way, but what kind of future would my daughters have in a country that hated white people. I had spent so much time in the squatter camps and locations. I knew first-hand the disadvantaged life my friends had to endure because of Apartheid. But reversing the hatred was not the solution. And unfortunately, that is exactly what was happening. I feared that in the future it would only get worse.

I spoke to Honey about moving to the U.S.A. Our relationship was pretty rocky at that point. After our second child, she started to smoke weed again. We were on different paths. And we were making a minimal effort to draw together. I think for her, a change seemed like a good idea too. A fresh start.

It was a long and drawn out process of paperwork. There were so many issues, the largest of which being my criminal record. Once again there was divine intervention. I managed to get my record expunged. That was an impossible task, made possible by the hand of God.

My parents were devastated. I mean, you can imagine. Their son finally cleans up his act. They had spent my whole life watching me throw it away. And now, finally, they had grandchildren. What a delight that was for them. And I was taking that all away from them. Of course, they understood. The kids needed a future. South Arica was not the place for that. But it was very hard never-the-less.

John 8

So if the Son sets you free, you will be free indeed...

39:
Land of the Free

America was different and the same simultaneously. We found a place to rent in Miami. The neighbourhood was Israeli. It's like all the Israeli people that moved to the states lived in this neighbourhood. The problem is they were all hustlers. Movers and shakers would do anything to make a buck.

We kept to ourselves. We both got jobs. I got quite a good job because of my experience at the airline. And Honey got a job working for some T.V. company.

We had some fun. In South Africa, things were very expensive. A person could save for years to get a good car. Here these things were very affordable. We had great cars, great electrical appliances. Life was great. We could afford the things we wanted. The kids were doing great in their new school.

One night Honey comes to me, "Listen, Dave, I'm going to fudge my sales sheet a bit."

"Don't" I say "Dishonesty brings repercussions,"

"But everyone is doing it, if I don't, I will look like the only one who is doing badly." She answered.

"Don't," I said again.

That was the end of the conversation. I thought no more of it. Until...

"I got fired today." That was Honey.

"Why?" I asked.

"I did it, the thing you said not to do."

Well, I blew up. For the first time in a very long time. Things would be so tight financially until she found another job. I enjoyed the way we were living. Not turning over every cent. Now it was going to get hard. I just hoped she found another job soon.

But she didn't. She was smoking weed daily. Just chilling at home. I took on more hours to pick up the deficit. Working 12 hours a day and weekends. I was feeling it too. Eventually, I organised her an interview for a job. She messed it up.

I was sure she did it on purpose. She enjoyed sitting at home smoking weed. The kids were at school most of the day. Resentment started creeping in. Our relationship started to deteriorate.

Ironically enough, putting in all those extra hours impressed my boss. I got a few promotions. Started earning the big bucks. I also started having the occasional beer. I mean I deserved it. I worked all the time. Barely got to see my family.

Money is a funny thing. It cost me to have it. Cost me time and my freedom and my peace of mind. Was costing me my marriage too. So I decided to bite the bullet and buy a house. After all, I was in my mid-thirties. I have a wife and two kids, a good time to own a home.

The real estate market was in a huge slump so I got a really good deal. Big house in a wonderful neighbourhood. Swimming pool, big garden, the American dream.

Some of the wiring and electronics needed some work. So I got a quote. Way too expensive. But I knew a guy, who knew a guy. He came and did the job for a third of the price. We hit it off from the word go, so at the end of the day I took him home and he invited me in for a beer. I had been drinking quite regularly at that point so I went in.

We're sitting in his garden, it's a beautiful evening. At this point, I have had a few beers. Just enjoying the evening and the company and the wind-down. His wife comes out, leans over him, puts something in his hand and kisses his cheek.

I wish I could tell you that I left at the point. I wish could say that I was strong enough to know better. I wish a lot of things...

He hit that crack pipe right in front of me. The old familiar smell hit my nostrils. I felt like I had been stranded on a deserted island for the last four years. Only able to eat berries and leaves. Then someone magicked me into a room with a buffet of the most glorious food in the world. Like something climbed out of my body and melted into that smell.

I didn't go home that night...

John 10

The thief comes to steal kill and destroy...

40:
The Thief

Satan was laughing. The devil himself was laughing at me. He watched me walk clean and straight for four years. He didn't even come along to tempt me. Maybe if he had, I would have been prepared for it. Like had a weapon or some armour.

The truth is, he was just waiting for that perfect moment. And it wasn't enough for him that I was back on crack. He had a lot more to offer.

When I got home Honey took one look at me and she knew. This was where our relationship began, and she was no fool. But she was a mother now; she had no interest in the hard stuff. She was livid with me.

Huge fight. She is screaming at me about having responsibilities and kids. I'm screaming that she just hangs around smoking weed on her lazy fat ass. Then she is telling me that if I continue down this road she will take the kids and leave.

I'd been up all night, not in the mood for her. I go to sleep.

So the road gets rocky, it gets slippery. In fact, there is so much trash on that road I can't even see where I am going.

We are fighting all the time now. I'm still holding on to my job. At first, I only smoked on the weekends. Then once during the week. You know how it goes. You tell yourself

Wednesday is okay because it's the middle of the week so you get your reward. Before you know it, I'm back to smoking every day.

The thing is, it wasn't like before. My conscience was killing me. Before I smoked because I thought I wanted to. But now I really didn't want to. I kept thinking about Jesus. About how much He forgave me for that day. He forgave a disgusting, violent criminal junkie. I mean I don't think I ever killed anyone, but it's not like I stopped to check. You don't stab a man in the neck; take his wallet and stick around to see if he is okay.

Jesus forgave all that. Not only that, He gave me light instead. He gave me joy and peace and freedom. And this is how I repay Him! I should have been out trying to help others. That's what the Bible says. But all I had been doing is looking at my own life. Trying to help myself. I just knew I was not good enough for Jesus. I mean who was I kidding. Jesus is for other people. People who can be good. I would never be able to be good.

The wife got so sick of me; she said she needed a break. She took the kids to visit her mother. They were away for 2 months. I was happy for it. I needed to get my head together. I was really trying hard to quit the crack. And I was doing quite well too...

Proverbs 5

For the lips of an adulterous woman drip honey, and her speech is smoother than oil...

41:
The Serpent

I was trying to clean up, I really was. For Honey, for the kids and most of all for Jesus. I mean even though I knew I was never going to be good enough for Him, at least wanted to show Him that I was grateful for what He gave me that day.

It was Saturday. I mowed the lawn, was enjoying a few beers while I did it. My phone rang. It was Kiara, a woman I used to work with. I can't tell you why she phoned that day. What I can tell you is that I was bored. I was tired of the quiet. So I invited her over.

Damn, I forgot how lush this woman was. Or maybe I just tell myself that. She was exotic and voluptuous. She had soft secret places I could just melt into. And she had the appetite and energy of a teenager. We couldn't get enough of each other.

My enemy knew that even though he got me to slip with the drugs, he was losing his power in that area. So he brought another vice. Lust. And it worked. I was loving every moment it. She was married, I was married, so it's wasn't going to get complicated either.

We had a lot of freedom. She popped in any time she felt like it. Day or night. Then one night she pops in and brings some a friend. Her friend brings a boyfriend. And as luck would have it, he is a crack dealer.

Black drug dealers hanging out in white neighbourhoods. Felt like I was back in Cape Town for a while.

Satan is laughing alright. I'm not only batting (smoking crack) full time. I'm also cheating on my wife with a married woman. This is not backsliding. This is diving headfirst into a bucket of sh*t!

The trouble was, I couldn't even smell the sh*t. I was blinded by my own lust. I had been starved in that area. Married to a nag who kept her legs crossed. I was an easy target in that area.

Of course, I know that the right thing to do is tough it out. Sort it out. Make long-term decisions for the sake of the kids. But I was just the kind of person who liked to distract myself from the issue. I'd been like that all my life. It's hard to teach an old dog new tricks. Not to mention the fact that the distraction was delicious.

Before you know it, Honey is back. Now I'm juggling too many balls and I don't have enough hands.

Honey is all over me. She expected to come back to a remorseful husband who had missed her and the kids so much. Instead, she could smell the bucket of sh*t that was sticking all over me. She is screaming divorce on a daily basis.

Kiara and I are meeting secretly. It was fun for a while. Nothing like stolen moments and hot sticky secrets to blind you from the truth. After a while, I get tired of worrying about Honey catching us or her husband catching us. The thrill is gone, so to speak. This isn't fun anymore and I want out. Not to mention the crack dealer who has taken a real shine to me. I'm his kind of people. But I am not supposed to be anymore.

Well, you can never keep all those balls in the air. Obviously, at some point, you gonna drop them. But you know I am a special kind of person. I decided to add a few more balls. You know, just for kicks!

I don't know what I was thinking. Clearly, I was not thinking. The truth is, I had a good life. I had a beautiful home. I had two princess daughters. They were so beautiful, like a breath of fresh air when they walked into the room.

But I was not focusing on the positive things in my life. I kept looking at the negative. And because of that, I drove myself to be unhappy. Which drove me to look for somewhere to drown my unhappiness. All of that from staring at only one side of the coin for too long.

2 Corinthians 11

...your minds may somehow be led astray from your sincere and pure devotion to Christ...

42: More Balls

What I'm going to tell you right now is the absolute truth. I kid you not. I really don't know what is wrong with me. Sometimes I think all those drugs I took made the sensible part of my mind fall out.

So here I am with all my balls in the air. The wife, the kids, the bit on the side, her husband, my drug problem and my conscience. My conscience was the worst. I knew Jesus was still here. I could feel Him. I was doing my darndest to chase Him away but it wasn't really working.

I am on my way to meet Kiara. Literally going to meet her for some afternoon sex. And I see this chick. Man, this woman is fine! FINE!

I can tell that she is a gym girl. She works out a lot. That body is defined and tight.

I go and chat with her for a bit and get her phone number. She is so hot it's all I can do not to call her as I'm walking away. When I see Kiara that day, I'm thinking about Natacha. I can't get her out of my mind. I touch Kiara and imagine its Natacha's skin. I look into Kiara's eyes and her beauty changes into the smutty face of an adulteress. She looks used and worn out. I want Natacha.

A few days later I call her, she tells me she is busy. Blows me off. What the hell, she seemed keen when we were chatting. Then another couple of days, she calls me. I get it. Power games. And she is one point up. I can't wait to see her.

And this is how it goes. Every time I want to see her she blows me off. Then calls at another time. I'm in a constant state of wanting more from her. More of her.

I move out from our beautiful big home and get an apartment. I just can't juggle anymore. I want her and only her. But the woman is elusive man. She is doing my head it. Power games all the time. And I am the constant loser.

Eventually, she agrees to move in with me. On the condition that there are no drugs. She doesn't like drugs. I'm so happy about this. Now she can't blow me off anymore. We will be living together. It was like I could finally get that elusive high. The one you chase your whole life.

But now that she is living with me, if I do something she doesn't like, she crosses her legs. And it seems I always doing something she didn't like. She was a hard woman to please.

She said no drugs and I honoured that. But I drank, and I drank a lot. I hid most of it from her. Like she would think I was having my first drink for the evening, meanwhile, I already had four on the way home.

It got so I felt like I couldn't do it anymore. I really loved Natacha, but I was not the kind of man who liked to feel confined. She confined, she dominated. Even Honey wasn't like that. I needed to feel free, even if I wasn't.

Next thing I know she is telling me she is pregnant and she is keeping it. A pregnant dominant woman. That was a lot of fun!

But when we found out it was a boy I was determined to make it work. I had two wonderful daughters and they were pure sunshine in my life. But a son carries your name. He is the head of the next generation. Plus it made me think so much about my own life. A girl's life is different to a boy. It's softer somehow.

I wanted my son to have a father figure that he could look up to, that he could rely on, and most of all that he could trust.

I loved my own parents, and I respected them a lot but they lied to me for a very long time. And the way the truth came out was just ugly. There is no other way to put it. Ugly. It hurt to know that my real mother didn't want me.

Did I mention that I found her? No, I don't think I did. Well, I did find her, but I had no interest in seeing her.

Natacha and my daughters get on well. She has a lot of energy, being a gym girl and all. They are all excited about the new baby. I think my daughters were too young to feel any kind of uncertainty about daddy having a baby with another woman. My oldest was 12 and she did ask a lot of questions. But once he was born they loved him to bits. It was like having a real live doll to play with.

I loved him to bits too. With his curly hair and his needy innocent stare. What an incredible feeling it was to have a son. Natacha was, is a good mother to him. But she is not the greatest girlfriend. We were not getting along at all.

The thing is, we did not communicate much. I had no idea what was going on inside her head. I mean I knew that things weren't great. But I didn't think it was that serious. I was still drinking a lot.

One day we get into a huge argument. I can't even remember what it was about. She tells me she is leaving. Taking our son. I didn't believe her. Where was she gonna go? It was just another argument you know? When you say stuff you don`t mean.

I was angry and needed to blow off some steam. I went out. Came back in the early hours of the morning.

Crept into the dark apartment, being as quiet as I could. I didn't want to wake my son, but I also didn't want to wake Natacha and her angry mouth.

I fell into a deep drunken sleep. When I woke they were gone. I was devastated! I didn't even know if they were already gone when I crept in that morning.

Genesis 3

Now the serpent was more crafty than any of the wild animals the Lord God had made. "Did God really say 'You must not eat from any tree in the garden'?" The woman said to the serpent "We may eat fruit from the trees in the garden, but God did say 'You must not eat fruit from the tree that is in the middle of the garden, and you must not touch it, or you will die.' "You will not certainly die," the serpent said to the woman "For God knows when you eat from it, your eyes will be opened, and you will be like God, knowing good and evil."

43: Biological Mother

I guess I should take a moment to talk about it. The truth is that I haven't wanted to. It's a painful subject. I can't begin to explain what it feels like when your own mother didn't want you.

I understand that there are always circumstances. Like the one girlfriend that I had who was also adopted. Her parents were junkies. I am sure the mother did not mean to fall pregnant. Perhaps she was unable to get an abortion. Perhaps she didn't want to go to a hospital. That would mean they would find out that she was using and try to help her. Maybe she didn't want that help. So she just stayed away from them.

In the end, she had to have the baby. I mean that's what happens after nine months. Maybe she looked at her daughter and felt all the love in the world. Maybe she knew that someone else would love her the same way. Someone who could offer her a life, a future. Maybe she knew that she would never be able to do those things. So she gave her child away, not because she didn't love her. But because she loved her that much.

We see and hear about things like this every day. But still. The logistics of it never changes the way we feel inside. Adopted children want to know who their parents are. They want to know why they weren't good enough. And yes, it doesn't mean that the child was not good enough. But that is the way it always feels. Even a newborn can smell its own mother's skin. Even a newborn knows when that smell is from another person. And they carry that. It's just the way it is.

I found out who my mother was in a time that I was still very angry. My girlfriend at the time really pushed for me to go and see her. But I knew it was a bad idea. I was always high or hanging. I would never be able to control my emotions. So I didn't go.

Maybe she saw that as me rejecting her. Maybe the pain of all of it was too much for her. You know? Like Pandora's Box? If you open it so much sh*t is gonna fly out you better just leave the lid on.

So I never did meet her. And I guess I never will. All I know about it is that she slept with the wrong man and was unable to keep me because of that.

It's very sad and I feel bad for her. I can't imagine what it must have been like. But I cannot feel responsibility for her emotions. I have my own to worry about on that subject.

I am very grateful to my adoptive parents for what they tried to do. They gave me a good life. And they stuck around even when I went right off the rails. It must have been so hard for them too. Having children ups the ante.

If you mess up and you have no kids, well you got a little wet. But if you mess up and you have kids, it's like a blinking tsunami.

2 Corinthians 4

...outwardly we are wasting away...

44:

Wasting Away

I was devastated! She took my son! He was only eight months old! He can't tell her if he misses me. He can't speak yet! When my daughter's miss me they tell Honey and she lets the see me. I can't accept this. I have to get them back!

I tried, man I tried had. But she would not come back. I could have brought her the moon she still would not have come back. But I wanted them back. I wanted my family back. I wanted my son back. It's the worst feeling you know when there is nothing you can do. You just can't get him back.

My apartment was so quiet. Too quiet. I started to avoid coming home. Went out straight after work. Women and booze. Lots of it. But eventually, I always had to go home. The silence screamed at me. The empty baby's room jam-packed with memories. The dirty kitchen wiped clean of any trace of Natacha.

I lost my appetite. I threw up a lot. Probably all the acid in my stomach. I lost weight. I lost a lot of weight. The mirror was looking dangerously close to Israel. But I didn't care.

The trouble with having a past like mine is this. Not being able to raise my son is a big thing. It would be a big thing for any man. But when something as big as this happens, all the other baggage comes tumbling out of the suitcase too.

I lost my son. I lost my daughters. I couldn't make it work with Honey. I couldn't make it work with Natacha. There is something wrong with me. Other men have good relationships. Even men from my background. So it's me.

I am the problem. What is wrong with me? Even my own mother didn't want me. And worst of all, I can't be a Christian. I am not even able to do that! The great book says everyone can do that.

I know that Jesus loves me. I felt it that day in church. It was overwhelming. His love washing over me in waves of light. But how do I live with that? How am I supposed to be the person He wants me to be. I just don't know.

He wants me to be good, but I will never be good enough. He wants me to be kind, but I will never be kind enough. He wants me to be gentle, but I will never be gentle enough. He wants me to be patient and forgiving and tolerant. But I don't know how to be all those things. The harder I try the more I fail.

I don't know how anybody manages to be all of those things. And all that happens is I get confused and feel guilty and rejected.

I don't know how my mother did it. I really cannot imagine it. To have a child and just give it away. I mean, I didn't carry my son in my belly. I didn't bring him into the world. But I can barely breathe for the pain of missing him.

Psalm 91

For He will command His angels concerning you, to guard you in all your ways...

45:
The Helicopter

I'm sure you have heard that story. There was a great storm which brought floods. People's cars were washing away down the streets. Everybody starts panicking. They find makeshift boasts. Frantically climbing into them so as to save themselves from drowning.

One man, a Christian, get on to the roof of his house. A makeshift boat comes past, a man calls out

"Hey get on here with us, you are going to drown!"

The Christian man replies,

"The Lord will save me."

A little while later a motorboat comes past.

"Hey, you" Come get in the boat! You are going to drown!"

The Christian man responds,

"The Lord will save me."

Finally, a rescue helicopter flies down. A man shouts through his loudspeaker.

"Grab the rope, you are going to drown!"

The Christian man shouts back,

"The Lord will save me!"

The Christian man drowns. When he gets to heaven he asks God 'why did you not save me?'

God replies "What are you talking about? I sent you a raft, a motorboat and a helicopter."

In my case, the good Lord skipped the raft and the motorboat. I guess he knew that I was in a bit more trouble than that. He went straight to the helicopter. Fortunately, I was wise enough to recognise that.

The helicopter was a woman. But not the kind of woman I usually had in my life. She was soft-spoken, patient, kind but also firm and very confident about herself.

She worked with me. I started to talk to her. Seek her out to talk to her. I really loved the way she listened. She was attentive, she never seemed to be thinking about what she wanted to say next. She actually gave all her attention to listening to me.

We started spending time together outside of work. She was a strong believer, her faith firmly set in God. She saw the world through a different set of eyes. She looked at things in a way I had never considered. She taught me innocence, purity, wholesomeness. Things I never knew about. She had never taken a drug in her life. Can you imagine that? This knowledge fascinated me. I had never met a woman who had never tried drugs. Not even a single one.

The other thing that drew me to her was the fact that she seemed to like me for me. All the women I had known in my life, were interested in me because I was a bad boy. But she was not that kind of woman, she had no agenda. She just genuinely liked me.

You can imagine how hard this was for me in the beginning. I kept looking for the agenda. I kept up my suspicious guard. But she was patient. And slowly but surely she broke down some of my walls. Walls I'd spent my entire life building.

She knew things. Things I had questions about. She taught me that God loves me because of His goodness, not because of mine. And that what Jesus did, paid for my sins. So I should never feel that I was not good enough for God.

Because never once did He ask me to earn it. In fact, He clearly said it's a free gift and all I have to do is receive it.

I had struggled with this for a long time. I really felt like I was not good enough. I had no idea that I didn't have to be. No one had to be. Because God knew that no one could be.

I began to understand that feeling guilty was a good thing. It meant that I actually wanted to please God. And that feeling was His conviction. Conviction is just Him saying, 'you can do better than that.' It's not condemnation. So I should just stop feeling guilty and say 'you are right, I can do better than this. Thank you for reminding me.'

Of course, it wasn't all roses. I still had serious addiction problems. I was still drinking so much. I had already lost about 20kgs. I was not overweight to begin with so that was a lot of weight.

We kept seeing each other. In a way it was hard for me. I was living two lives. I loved being with her, but I also loved my drink. I loved what she represented. She was so pure. But I could not bring myself to stop my evil habits.

Eventually she moved in with me. She didn't like the idea from her Christian point. But she was just as drawn to me as

I was to her. Neither of us wanted to be apart for long periods of time. So it seemed logical to live together.

Psalm 68

God sets the lonely in families; he leads out the prisoners with singing. But the rebellious live in a sun-scorched land.

46: Freedom

It was a Friday. I remember that quite clearly. Vee went to work. I had the day off. I was kind of restless and bored so I have a few drinks. It was only ten in the morning. The drinks weren't really helping that restless feeling. I scroll through my phone. I see the number of a guy I met a few years ago. I don't know if he still has the same number, but if he does I can probably score some weed off him.

I phone him, he tells me he has no weed but he has something better. Even though I'd had a few drinks I drive to his place. He hands me a rock!

Mother fu*er, I had not touched that stuff in years. I was nervous about it, but I was not going to say no. So there it was. I was on crack again.

I tried to hide it from Vee. I'd wait until she went to bed and then bat the whole night. This worked for a while. One day she came out on the balcony and caught me. I was a bit shocked to see her and tried to remove my pipe from her sight.

"Let me see," she said.

So I hit the pipe again, right in front of her.

Afterwards, she sat down next to me and pulled me into her embrace. She rocked me a bit, almost like a child, and started singing Amazing Grace. Inside myself, I went all the way back to the church with Sonny. When she was finished singing she started to pray. She prayed in a language I did not recognise.

Something changed in me that day.

This woman gave me unconditional love. Something I had never experienced in my life. She did not judge me. Again, something new.

A few years later

I look down at my key ring. 'JUST FOR TODAY'

That's what it says. I had always thought that AA or NA or any other anonymous group was a bunch of nonsense. Turns out I was wrong.

Vee and I got married. We are still married. We are happy. She is my angel, my helicopter. Sure we have our ups and downs, who doesn't? But all of that is something on the surface. I have roots with this woman. Strong roots.

You know, she even encouraged me to find my biological siblings. And I did find them. I have chatted with them over social media. They are still in South Africa. I feel like I finally belong.

It's been a hell of a journey, but one thing I know.

GOD NEVER LEFT MY SIDE

Author's Note

I never met David personally. We connected through social media. He knew I was a Christian author and mentioned that he had quite the story to tell. I offered to write it if he ever felt inclined to tell it.

I had no idea what his story was.

Once he started sharing it, I was blown away. This man is brutally honest! He doesn't seem to mind if the truth makes him look bad. He just values the truth that much. So do I!

I'd prefer a hurtful truth than a sugar-coated lie any day of the week. This man has my absolute respect in that area.

The second thing that struck me about him is his loyalty. I had the pleasure of meeting a friend of his, through social media again. The loyalty between these two men is something movies are made of. I don't think I have ever seen it in real life.

Loyalty and honesty are words freely thrown around but seldom acted upon. It takes a deep level of commitment to actually live by those two words. A level few manage to hold on to.

David is an outstanding and determined man, with the softest heart. This is what makes him the powerful warrior he is today. A warrior for Christ!

I'm pleased to say that in the process of writing this book, we procured a friendship. Based on the deep and intimate truth he had to share in order for me to do my part, and out of our mutual love for Jesus. I believe it is a friendship that will last a lifetime.

I am going take up a little bit more of your time over the next few chapters because I believe that some of you must have questions.

If you are a fellow believer then maybe you relate to David's story. Maybe you had some kind of revelation of God that turned you into a believer but after that, you just couldn't seem to make it work out. And somehow you just feel lost and frustrated.

Or maybe you are not a believer at all. And somehow this testimony has not managed to convince you that Jesus is alive. I assure you that He is alive and well and just waiting to give you all that He died for.

The Clouds

Say you are sitting on your sofa. You are watching television. You get up to go to the kitchen, you're thirsty. The kitchen window is open and you just stop and stare.

The moon is full. It's so full it's huge, it's mesmerising...pregnant...bursting with incredible light. You stand at your window, soaking in the beauty...it makes you feel...something unexplainable...different...awesome. I sucks you in. It makes you feel that you are part of something and is not from here...part of something supernatural...miraculous...shifting places inside of you...

Eventually, you go back to the couch and watch some more television. Initially, the glow of what you just experienced is still there. You feel a warm haze around you but then the T.V. show sucks you in again and you forget about the moon.

When you get up to go to bed, you remember it again. So you go back to the window have one last look. But a big grey cloud has covered the moon. All you can see is the beautiful light shining around the edges of the cloud. You feel disappointed.

'Oh well,' you think' it was a nice moment.'

So let's take a closer look at that analogy.

The moon is God, the light in the darkness.

The television is Satan, the worldly distraction.

So God revealed His light to you. At that moment you repented. He delivered you from your demon. The one that influenced and compelled you in a direction you did not want to go but felt you had no control of.

This is usually something that you considered a big sin. For some, it might have been as simple as using profanity constantly or gossiping about people. For others, it might have been drugs or alcohol. Maybe violence or adultery. But whatever it was, after you had your revelation of God, you changed that thing. Or to be precise He changed that thing.

But what about the rest of your life? You see, you went back to the couch with a warm haze, but did you change the channel on the T.V.? No, you didn't. Satan knew that. So he also knew that he was going to get back in.

Matthew 12: When an unclean spirit comes out of a man, it passes through arid places, seeking rest and does not find it. Then it says 'I will return to the house I left.' On its arrival, it finds the house vacant, swept clean and put in order. Then it goes and brings with it seven other spirits more evil than itself, and they go in and dwell there. And the final plight of that man is worse than the first.

We cannot think that by getting rid of our 'big sin' we have done enough. If we don't change the channel i.e. our mindset, Satan will come back with his seven evil friends and move in!

For every single problem you have in your life, the answer is in the Bible. But how often do we look for the answer in the Bible? We go to friends for answers. (Psalm1: Blessed is the man who does not follow the advice of the wicked...)

Are you taking your problems to a strong person of faith or are you just speaking to Joe Soap from next door? We search for answers anywhere and everywhere. But we never go to the Bible! And we wonder why our troubles remain.

When Jesus said that the unclean spirit comes back and finds the house swept clean, He means that our heads are empty. They need to be filled with the Word of God! That is the ONLY thing Satan is afraid of.

Satan knows that God is real. Satan also knows the rules. Satan is allowed to come back if we invite him in. We may not know that we are doing it. But that is irrelevant to Satan. It's our own fault if we don't know. It's all in the Bible! There is nothing to stop us from reading it and informing ourselves.

How to Fill the House

If the house was full of the Word of God, we would not need to go back to the window and look at the moon a second time. The warm haze would have remained with us.

The warm haze is the Holy Spirit. When we grieve it, we can't feel it anymore. If we can't feel it, we can't hear it. And that is when we start walking in the wrong direction.

Proverbs 4: My son, attend to my words. Incline thine ear unto my sayings. Let them not depart from thine eyes. Keep them in the midst of thine heart. For they are life to those that find them and health to all of their flesh.

We are instructed to keep the Word of God alive in our minds and hearts. When must we do this? Always! If we don't do it, Satan has every right to come back into the clean house. It's as simple as that.

The Bible tells us to be careful about what we see and hear. It tells us to watch our tongues.

What are you looking at?

Age restricted movies with violence and sex? Scantly clad women? Friends smoking weed or drinking? Porn?

What are you listening to?

Music where the lyrics belong to Satan? Music from back in another time where you thought you were having more fun? Music that triggers certain emotions which are not Godly? Gossip? Rude and jesting jokes at the expense of others?

What are you speaking about?

Negative words that bring you down? Gossiping about other people? Profanity and rude jokes?

It sounds like a lot doesn't it? How can we do this? Be perfect people? We can't! But Jesus can!

I will give you two simple tips.

First. If you do any of these things, say sorry and mean it!

Second. If you don't know the Bible well enough just memorize one scripture and use that to replace any thought that will grieve your Holy Spirit.

The scripture I used before I knew the Bible was found in

2 Corinthians 10.

Actually, let me quickly take a moment to tell how I came to that scripture. I asked God. I said 'Lord, if I had to commit to memory just one scripture in the entire Bible, which one would you tell me to memorize.' He said 2 Corinthians 10.

When I say God, I mean the still, soft voice of the Holy Spirit.

So here it is.

For the weapons of our warfare are not carnal but spiritual, for the mighty destruction of strongholds. In so much as we refute all arguments, reasonings and every proud and lofty thing that sets itself up against the true knowledge of God. Taking every thought and purpose captive into the obedience of Christ.

You see, if we take our thoughts and purpose and make them captive to the obedience of Christ, we cannot be led astray!

Some examples.

Flesh: Geez that cashier is a bossy bit*h. When I get to the till I'm going to take as long as I can finding the small change. Just to irritate her.

Holy Spirit: That cashier looks very flustered. Be extra nice to her and leave her your small change. She is having a hard day.

Flesh: Sitting with some friends at lunch break and a revealingly dressed woman walks past. Your friend says 'look at those knockers, don't you just want to bury your face in there?' Flesh makes a slurping vibrating sound.

Holy Spirit: Walk away from this conversation. That is someone's daughter, someone's mother someone's sister. It could be your daughter one day.

Distant Deity

So what is the bottom line in all this?

You have two options.

Either you say, okay I believe in Jesus Christ. If you do, your salvation is procured. Your name is written in the lamb's book of life. So just go on as you were and wait for the day you meet your maker. You have a distant Deity that you speak to every now and then. Of course, if you take this option you have to accept that everything in your life is due to your own choices. The condition of your marriage or your health. Your income or lack of it. And you will have to pray for a lot of discernment because many times you can get exactly what you want. But it's not from God. It's from Satan. And he gives it because he knows it will keep his grip on you. Don't worry, you will still go to heaven but your time on earth may not be all that could have been.

Or.

You submit your life to God. You have a personal relationship with Him. You take His book of instructions and you read it and apply it to your life. Then He can direct your steps. He can take all responsibility for your life. He can level mountains and provide for your every need. Only if you commit to Him. Your level of commitment is directly proportional to the level of responsibility He takes for your life.

I'll be honest. In the beginning, it's going to feel like you are walking against the wind. But the more you apply his

Word to your life, the less you will notice the wind. Your mind cannot be renewed in a day. But if you start today and keep going, you will get there! Every day you delay is one less day on your journey.

Just understand this. You cannot have both! God will not be mocked! Don't think that you can somehow half commit. He will not meet you there. I say that with absolute certainty because it's in the Bible. And every word of the Bible is God-breathed. (2 Timothy 3)

Jesus said He spews out lukewarm! Remember that!

Two nights ago I was watching a movie, I wasn't concentrating because I was thinking about this book. I asked God what it is that He wants me to relay. He said 'Trust in me and lean not on your own understanding.'

I got up and went to write it down.

Our own understanding and reasoning is very often our downfall. Satan uses it all the time. In fact, I believe that the seven more evil friends that Jesus spoke of, are the subtle demons. The ones we don't notice. They have much more power.

Our own understanding and reasoning:

She is better than your wife, she is younger and hotter. Go for her. Satan is the master of lust.

Trusting God:

She will destroy your life which is why Satan wants you to go there. It doesn't matter if your marriage seems stale, Trust God!

Our own understanding and reasoning:

Wow, what a blessing that I found this wallet. And it has so much money in it. I am so short at the moment.

Trusting God:

Give it back to the owner. God will triple that blessing if you do the right thing!

Satan always has the short term answer. Because we humans are impatient. Satan's solution is always appealing.

God mostly takes the long way round, because He wants something in us to change. Change for the better. That usually takes time.

Now I'm going to tell you something. You may read this and think, okay I want God's will for my life. I want Him to level mountains for me. I want His provisions. I am going to start reading the Bible. I am going to start replacing bad thoughts with His Word.

But then somehow you don't feel like it. It feels like an effort. Too much effort. That my friends is Satan. Forget about how you feel and do it anyway. Do it because that is what it takes.

Resist the devil and he will flee!

Standing in front of you are two pot plants. The one you water is the one that will grow. Choose Satan's ways and the flesh will grow.

Choose God's ways and the spirit will grow.

Psalm 37

Delight yourself in the Lord and He will give you the desires of your heart

Some Words from David

I had this idea of writing down my life story for while - the place in my life I am at now consists a lot of motivating people - in my job and also on a personal level - fitness, wellness, etc.

Then I thought maybe my story will give even if only 1 person hope from the hell they find themselves in - does not necessarily drugs - whatever the addiction is - porn, food, alcohol, money, etc - there is hope to overcome - to win so to speak in life - we don't have to be defeated...

And also of course - "why am I still alive" - should have been dead so many times - so many times - or locked up for a long time- whichever way death would have come by bullet or overdose - I would have lost - being on the wrong path - going in the wrong direction...maybe my life of hell did serve a purpose - there is nothing coincidental about anything that happens - we have the option as to which direction we will go or which choice we will make...

The things I have been exposed to and have seen have opened my eyes - literally - a different outlook on life where once you are living in the light, you can identify darkness immediately - no one is able to con you - pull wool over your eyes so to speak...

So I headed out on this journey - I thought hey - it will be easy - but easy it wasn't

- to be reminded of all that again and be shamed was hard - It was like being tortured and tormented by those demons again - them reminding me of my mistakes and sin - at times it was unbearable - who would have thought writing down your story would be this painful - but you know what, it was worth it - it was a time of spiritual growth again and getting more mature in my walk - it was also closure - so many things that were just covered up and never addressed - I had to address each one of the ones written down and also the ones I have omitted(oh yes there are a few omissions) I had to ask for forgiveness for.

I want to take this opportunity to ASK EVERYONE and their families I have ever wronged, hurt, sold drugs to or deceived, for forgiveness - I know it's hard to forgive someone like me, however, I would really like you to try - please.

SO I leave you, the reader with this - life is short, not all of us get second chances, take full hold of whatever it is you are doing in your life and live it for good - we change when we stop focusing on ourselves and look to help others.

One of my favourite quotes - is by James Dean - "Dream as if you'll live forever, live as if you'll die today" - keep it simple - don't' sweat the small stuff...

Bless you, in the name of Yeshua Ha Mashiach...

Other books by this author

Here There and Everywhere   the boy with the gifted eyes

Here There and Everywhere   the boy who hears the shadows

Here There and Everywhere   the man who saw the future

Down to the Top

Convinced

Where Darkness isn't Dark

Living in the unseen world

The years the Locusts have stolen

I will walk in Freedom

God's Ice-Cream

Bronsky the bat

Yellow banana the banana split

Sneak Peek

Convinced

Have you ever noticed that when people see a car wreck ahead they almost always slow down to get a closer look? It's like somewhere inside of us there is this morbid sense of curiosity. A strange unexplained desire to look at the bleeding dying people. I'm sure some people even feel guilty about it afterwards. Wondering why they would want to look at something like that. Wondering if there is something wrong with them.

The truth is there is nothing wrong with it. Bar mental illness, nobody wants to die. So we feel the need to look because it reminds us of the value of life and how quickly it can end. It is morbid, but our curiosity stems from the fact that we think it's always going to happen to someone else. We feel safe looking at such things. If your loved one were lying there you wouldn't want to look. The fact that they are strangers seems to make it okay. It's almost like watching the news on the television.

Every time I meet a person that was institutionalised as a child. Or one who grew up in multiple foster homes. My first thought is 'I wonder if they were sexually abused.' I'm sure most people think that very same thing. There certainly are enough movies made about that sordid subject. It's the car wreck slow down drive by. People want to know. It's just the way it is.

So was I sexually abused?

The answer is yes, yes I was. The car wreck slow down drive by is that I would lie in bed at night staring at the sliver of light coming from under the closed door. Wishing and hoping that the dreaded shadow would not appear.

When the shadow did appear I would screw my eyes closed as tightly as possible. I would bury myself in the blankets, thinking, wishing that he just wouldn't see me. But he always saw me, no matter how tightly I screwed my eyes closed. No matter how deep I buried myself in those blankets. He always saw me. Then I would feel his cold, dirty paedophile hands creeping onto my body.

That is the car wreck slow down drive by version of events. Nobody gets every detail on a drive by like that. I know it may seem that I'm being blasé. It's a defence mechanism.

Too many details are too much to bear. It doesn't hurt the man I am now, but it makes my heart bleed for that child. The child I used to be.

Printed in Great Britain
by Amazon